Seven Pennies
In My Hand

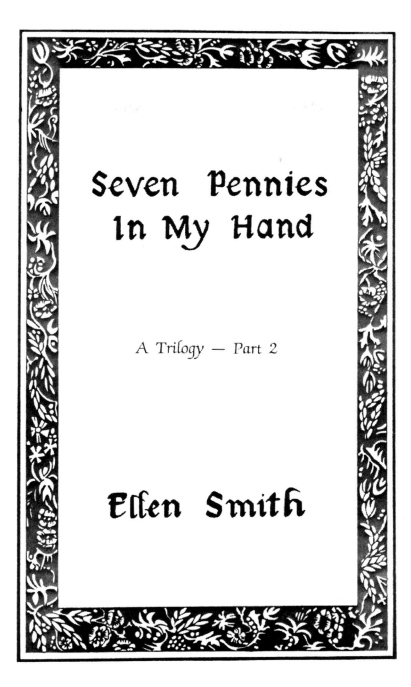

Seven Pennies In My Hand

A Trilogy — Part 2

Ellen Smith

Seven Pennies in my Hand
Ellen Smith

First edition published by author 1984

Second edition published by Heart of Albion Press
on behalf of Wymeswold Church Appeal Fund 2005.

ISBN 1 872883 87 7

Illustrations by Susan Jalland
Cover and title page by Gaynor Smith

Heart of Albion Press
2 Cross Hill Close, Wymeswold
Loughborough, LE12 6UJ

albion@indigogroup.co.uk

Visit our Web site: www.hoap.co.uk

Printed in England by Booksprint

To my beloved husband
in memory of
our happy years together.

Contents

FOREWORD

This second part of my life story covers the early years of my marriage, from 1931 to 1945, when we farmed in the same old way as the two generations before us. We worked exceedingly hard during the Second World War but, despite much sadness, we managed to enjoy many happy experiences, including the birth of my third son, Michael.

I am grateful to all those who have helped in the production of this book – my friend Susan Jalland who did the illustrations, my granddaughter Gaynor Smith who designed the cover and the title page, Annmarie Amberg who typed the final text, and Annie Delin and my son David who looked after the editing. I must also express my appreciation to all those readers who have told me how they enjoyed my first book *Memories of a Country Girlhood*.

My third book will cover the rest of our farming years when modern methods replaced the old ones.

Wymeswold, 14 March 1984

1 MOVING INTO THE FARM

It was on Good Friday in the year 1934 that Sid and I moved into the farm, along with our two small sons, John Sidney and David Warner. Though my husband's father and his great-uncle John had farmed there for two generations, they had not given the place a name. This was a great inconvenience, as we were constantly getting other people's letters. Smith is a common name and there were many people called Smith living in our Leicestershire village of Wymeswold, whose streets had no numbers in those days. So we decided we must have a name for our farm. Many suggestions were made, but in the end we decided to call it 'Wysall Lane End Farm'. The house stood foursquare on a corner where two roads led out of the village. The front faced on to the Willoughby Lane (now East Road), but the side of the house, the farm entrance and access to most of our land were on Wysall Lane.

Since our marriage, when we lived in an old world cottage in Brook Street, both Sid and I worked extremely hard to pay for the live and dead farming stock owned by his father. Sid had earned extra money at night with the help of his father's horses, carting manure and anything else people needed moving. I well remember that the charge he made for the horses and cart, including his time for loading and unloading, was two shillings and sixpence, now twelve and a half pence.

I continued with my dressmaking, having had quite a good business in that line prior to my marriage. Between us we managed to pay his father for everything. He did not charge us any tenant right, as Sid had worked without wages on the farm since leaving school, which was the usual thing in those days. Nevertheless we were left with only a few pounds between us to start our farming lives. We faced a tremendous challenge, but we enjoyed every moment of it during those hard-working years.

Trinity College, Cambridge, which owned the farm, reduced the rent for two years, after which it was raised to slightly more than Sid's father had paid. The reduction of rent was a tremendous help, enabling us to get on our feet. Trinity College owned most of the Wymeswold farms and the tenants found them exceedingly good landlords. They also owned the vicarage at that time and always kept the chancel in the beautiful church of St Mary's in good repair.

We were many months settling into our farmhouse. One reason was because electric light was being installed, necessitating redecorating in every room. This took time, as there were five bedrooms and three large rooms downstairs. We knew there would be no money to spare for labour on this job, so I had to tackle it myself and earn the money by dressmaking to buy the paint and wallpaper. I was a complete novice at decorating but each room I did taught me new things – one learns by one's mistakes. By the time it was our sitting room's turn, I had got quite professional and made a grand job of it. During our thirty-odd years living at the farm, I was proud that I had redecorated the whole house three times.

Our herd of around fourteen milking cows and one hundred laying hens provided us with ready money from milk and eggs, some of which we sold at the farmhouse door. Sid and his brother Bob, who stayed to work on the farm after his father retired, used to be up in the morning before six o'clock. By half past seven they had finished the milking in readiness for the milk lorry, which had to get the milk into Nottingham every morning by around nine o'clock.

In summer, timing was very important, as the heat soon turned the milk sour. Nowadays, with refrigeration, timing is not quite so important, and the milk is collected in tankers, not churns. During the summer months, there was often a glut of milk, and it was not unusual for a full churn of milk to be sent back to us, the excuse being that it was sour. Now we were not fools, we knew when milk was sour, and I complained about the return of perfectly good milk. We were told by the lorry driver: "You won't get owt back, Missus. You have to have your turn as well as all the other farmers in getting your milk back when we have more than we can sell. You can gi' it to your pigs, Missus. We canner, not in the towns."

We never wasted this returned milk. Sid's father was an old hand at making Stilton cheese, and as we had the old slate vats down in the dairies still intact, he would make a couple of Stiltons which, when ripened, were really good. Sometimes I would make cream cheeses, but these had to be eaten quite soon or they would ripen and would quite literally run off the plates. My father loved them when they reached the runny consistency and quite often had one taken to him.

Besides cows and poultry, we kept pigs. Sid really loved looking after pigs and many a story could be told about them, like the time one sow had twenty piglets but only fourteen teats. Now it is not generally known, outside experienced pig farmers, that in a litter of newborn pigs each fights for the teat it prefers, leaving the weaker ones to accept what is left. This meant that twenty piglets could not survive, if left to fight it out for themselves.

Sid hated the thought of killing six of the piglets, so he solved the problem by taking half of them away from the mother, placing them in another sty, then with a deal of trouble, exchanging the piglets every four hours. Some mother sows would never accept this way of feeding their babies but this particular one did. For a fortnight Sid got up every night around two o'clock to change the piglets. This experiment was very successful, as after a fortnight they were drinking milk out of small trough and Sid was able to let ten stay with their mother. The other ten did quite well on cow's milk, but they did not look quite so well as those who had their mother's milk. Sid used to say: "They don't have quite the same bloom on them, Nell."

It is quite apt to describe a stubborn person as 'pig-headed', for a pig is the most stubborn animal on the farm, especially when it is being forced to do something it does not want to do. Sid would always try to persuade a pig, he rarely tried force.

At the same time pigs have quite a good brain. We had a huge pig we called Alice. I have seen Alice lift two huge heavy farm gates off their hinges with her nose to get back to piglets who were squealing blue murder while they were being castrated. Yet she was the most gentle and careful mother. I was fascinated to watch her feed her piglets. She would first carefully set her huge body on her tummy. Then, with her babies squealing hungrily around her, she would turn over inch by inch on to her side until she was in a position to feed them.

Many mother pigs were careless in lying down to feed their young. Sometimes as many as half the litter would be suffocated by the mother lying on them. When we found we had a mother of this kind, Sid would sit up for two or three nights in the sty to be there in readiness to save the piglets. He would sleep a lot of the time, of course, but a piglet that is fast under its mother's body keeps on squealing until the breath is all squeezed out of it. I have often saved a piglet during the daytime when hearing that particular kind of squeal. Nowadays the mother pigs are put into a kind of crate, thus minimizing deaths through lying on their babies. Many people think this way is cruel to the mother pig.

Day-old piglets can be just as stubborn as older ones, like one we named Georgie who was born along with twelve brothers and sisters. His mother had fourteen teats, one of which was a dud with little or no milk, which left thirteen good teats for thirteen strong little piglets. But Georgie chose the dud teat, and in spite of all our efforts at taking him away from it and placing him to the remaining good one, he would have none of it, fighting his way back to his chosen teat. Piglets always stick to one teat. Georgie became so thin and weak we decided to force-feed him by putting his nose into a cup of cow's milk, but he fought us all the way, so we started spooning it down his throat. After a few days, he capitulated and drank out of the cup. Afterwards he became quite tame, so much so that when we called 'Georgie', he came rushing to the door for his cow's milk.

We had another pig who had a mania for eating any piece of clothing she could get hold of. On washday we had to make sure she was shut up in her sty, otherwise she would reach up to the washed clothes and chew as many as she could. We could not leave any coats around, as she would even climb into the milk float and eat any coat left therein.

In those days we took our milk to the cheese factory. After emptying the churns, Sid would fill them up with whey which, when mixed with the meal, the pigs loved. They did well on this mixture, and our profits from pigs, milk and eggs kept us going financially until we received our first corn cheque. That first year's harvest was especially good, which proved lucky for us, as a bad harvest would have crippled us financially for several years.

When we first took over the tenancy from Sid's father, we continued to do everything in the same old way his father had done all those years ago. Every bit of work was done by men and horses. We had no tractors in those days, but oh, how everyone worked!

Grass was cut with a horse-drawn mowing machine, a brand new one which had taken practically my last pound of dress-making money to buy. We turned the grass by hand using a hay fork, but after a few years we managed to buy a swath-turner which saved many hours of back-breaking work. When the grass was ready, we used a horse-drawn rake which soon had the field in long rows of beautifully smelling hay. I used to love to watch the men, using just a hay fork, expertly gathering a huge amount of hay and tossing it up to another man waiting on the cart to receive it. When the load reached an enormous height, it was fascinating to see the dextrous handling of such great forkfuls of hay, which were put in exactly the right place to make a load safe for its journey to the stack yard.

The man who raised the stack also had to be an expert, otherwise it would not stand the winter. My father, who had started farming

during the First World War when his building trade was restricted to repair work, once had a stack of hay badly put together. Not only did the stack fall over, but it fell on some sheep sheltering from the wind, killing them.

Nowadays hay is baled and put under Dutch barns, safe from the weather, without the expert thatching needed when we first started farming. People my age feel great nostalgia when reminiscing about the years of the horse and cart, the meals eaten in the fields to save time going back to the farmhouse, and the glorious feeling one had when the last load arrived safely in the stack yard.

We did not make silage for our cattle, but we grew a whole field of turnips and mangolds. To grow these, a lot of work was needed. While Sid and his brother Bob hoed the rows, Bob's wife and I did the singling. The men left small patches of seedlings in each row about ten inches apart, and it was our job to pull out all the seedlings but the one we thought was the strongest. It was back-breaking tedious work, but we made it more interesting by having Sid and myself compete against Bob and his wife, the men betting a small amount as to which pair of us would finish the row first. There was certainly method in this madness, as we worked so hard the field was finished in record time, and I loved it.

The corn was harvested in the same way as the hay. We called the machine that cut the corn a binder. Some called it a reaper, but I liked the name binder because, after cutting the corn, this machine tied the sheaves with binder twine, dropping them neatly on to the ground. Then the men followed, picking up the sheaves and making them into stooks which were left until the corn was dry enough to stack.

It was a grand sight, a field full of stooks with the sun shining on them, but sometimes during inclement weather, with the rain seeming never to stop, the corn deteriorated daily, ending with it black and sprouting again. Fortunately this was rarely the case; mostly we saw our corn safely stacked and thatched, waiting for the

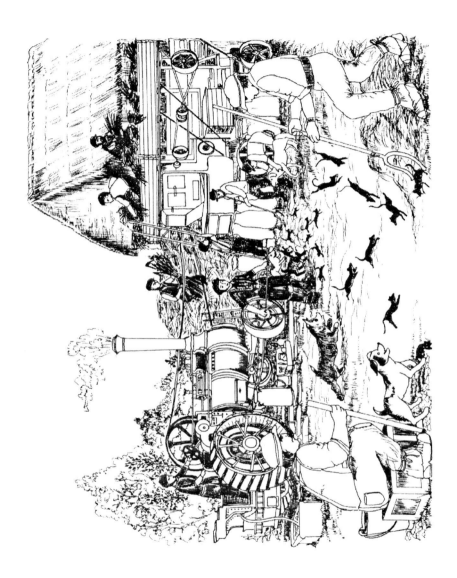

threshing machine which travelled round the district all through the winter, visiting each farm in its turn.

Threshing days were hard work for both the men and the farmers' wives. When we first started in the farm, most of the threshers came into the house for dinner. We cooked a huge joint of beef with baked potatoes, mashed potatoes and greens, with lashings of rich gravy and Yorkshire puddings, followed by apple pies. One had to see to believe the mess those men left: straw and chaff all over the room. There were no vacuum cleaners in those days. In later years this practice discontinued: only bread and cheese and beer were taken into the stack yard in the mid-morning, and tea and cakes in the mid-afternoon.

Each man was a specialist at his particular job, keeping pace with the others. A man named Mr Morris was in charge of the huge steam threshing machine. He and his mate came very early in the morning to set up the machine and get the fire going in order to heat the water.

When the bottom of the stack was reached, great sport was anticipated, because the army of rats which had made their home there all tried to escape. Trouser bottoms were tied up with string, as it was not unknown for the odd rat to try to take refuge up the trouser leg, which was a horrible experience. Every man who owned a dog brought it. The dogs knew by experience when the rats were due out, getting excited almost beyond control. One man named Sammy Clark, a regular follower of the threshing machine who generally worked on the stack, was an absolute pro at spearing a rat with his hay fork. No one could equal his prowess at this hard task, although many times I heard him telling the men how it was done – not by jabbing the fork at the rat but by drawing the tines across its back as it ran. He used to have a great inimitable laugh and each kill was accompanied by this 'Ha Ha Ha'. Years later, my son David often relates the story of Sammy the rat killer. I often wish we could have filmed the latter part of a day's threshing, with the stack becoming low, the men and dogs waiting, then the rush of rats trying to escape, and finally the kill – but those days are gone never to return. Sometimes I wonder what my grandchildren's children will think of our way of farming, when they put a tractor and plough in a field and the job is done by remote control, not to mention the huge combine harvesters which clear a field of corn and take the harvest into the mill all in one day.

A few years before we bought our own combine harvester, we had bought a second-hand threshing drum which was driven by a tractor. This threshed our corn quite satisfactorily, but when the new combine harvester arrived, making the old drum obsolete and practically worthless, we burnt it in a field, selling the scrap iron that was left. Now, as farm antiques, they have become extremely valuable to own. One in good condition has been known to make £20,000 in a farm sale. I shudder to think of burning that old threshing drum.

During those early years of haymaking and harvesting farmers' wives worked harder than most other women, from early morning till late at night. In my own case I was up at daylight to clean up the house. Then I cooked an egg and bacon breakfast for the family. During breakfast I would learn how many men would be working in our fields, all of whom would need a hot dinner. Sometimes there would be as many as thirteen or fourteen friends and neighbours helping to bring in the harvest. I would go into the garden, dig up the potatoes, gather the peas and beans, then pod the peas, cut up the beans, and peel the potatoes. The meat was always round of beef or leg of lamb. For pudding I usually made pies of various fruits. Before dishing up this huge dinner, I would line two huge butter baskets with newspaper which had previously been warmed in the oven, then fill the dishes with vegetables, a large jar of gravy and the huge joint of meat. The second basket would be filled with hot plates and the fruit pies. These baskets, when filled, weighed more than one woman should carry, and sometimes I had to struggle the best part of a mile before reaching the field where the men were working. But I was young and strong and oh the joy of seeing those hungry hard-working men tuck into their hot dinner! After a short rest in the field I would gather the dirty dishes and wend my way home to wash up the mountain of pots and pans. Then it was time to cut up two or three loaves of bread for sandwiches – we had no sliced loaves in those days – for the men's tea. Cakes were got ready, too, and tea brewed in a two-gallon can. Off I went to the fields again, a heavy basket in one hand and this huge tin can in the other. When my children were older, they would help carry these heavy loads. Sometimes, when needed, I would then help with the haymaking, or bring the cows from their pasture down to the farm, and tie them up ready for milking.

Milking a cow was one of the things I never mastered. I tried many times to learn but always failed miserably. When I saw other farmers' wives milking a cow, I used to feel quite jealous, but I felt I made up for this weakness by doing some things they could not, like making ginger beer which was taken into the field in huge stone bottles and placed in the dykes or under hedgerows to keep cool.

When work was done for the day, often as late as eleven o'clock at night, the men would troop into the large farmhouse kitchen, have a good wash at the sink, then sit down to a good supper of home-cured ham, with cheese to follow, which quite often was home-made cream cheese. While the men rested and chattered, I would clear up the table and tackle one more huge washing-up. Then, tired but completely happy, we would all say goodnight and make our way up to bed, hoping for a restful night, without cows or pigs giving birth, which would sometimes keep us awake for many hours.

When we bought our first tractor, I was allowed to have the pony and float to carry these heavy meals. After the war, when new machinery did the work of many men and horses, meals in the fields became unnecessary and women's work was considerably lightened, but I look back on those happy meals listening to the men chatting and teasing each other as to who could do this and that better and quicker than anyone else, and which could lift the heavier weight and so on.

Farming in my young days was such hard work that we started the winter looking forward to the long evenings together by the side of a huge fire of logs. I also caught up with my dressmaking orders, not to mention the making of rag rugs. The children and Sid helped to cut up the old coats and any other unwanted material suitable for rug making, while I was busy working out a pattern on the canvas ready for the start of pegging. Sid and I used to see who could work the most squares in one evening. By this method we certainly covered more ground, or should I say more canvas? I loved those long winter evenings, sewing, reading, rug making and playing cards. I look back on those early years on the farm with grateful thanks for such love and happiness.

2 VILLAGE CHARACTERS

In our village there was a gentleman named Mr White who kept a small pub called 'The Hammer and Pincers', which stood on East Road next door but one to our farm. He served as a stretcher-bearer through the First World War and, having a natural aptitude for first aid work, he became almost a professional. Many people had more faith in Mr White than in their own doctors, and in those days one had to pay a doctor for every call he made. The result was they went to see Mr White with injured limbs and small ailments. A saying in the village was: "Go and see Mr White. He can do you a lot of good and certainly won't do you any harm, and he will soon tell you if you need a doctor." I never knew Mr White to charge anyone for the help he gave, even though it must have cost him something for ointments and bandages, but he will be remembered by the people of Wymeswold for his goodness. When National Insurance became law, people like Mr White gradually became less used, as doctors' visits were made free and one was paid a sum of money each week during illness.

We also had a man called Cecil Mills who was a wizard with animals. Many a time, day or night, the farmers would fetch Cecil to their sick animals. With sheep he was particularly clever, saving many of their lives, especially at lambing time. Mr Mills made no charge: he did this work for the sheer love of it, saving a farmer many a vet's bill. A vet would have had to travel five miles on horseback or in his horse and gig.

When I was young, we had a town crier. Whenever his bell was heard in the streets, everyone rushed out to hear the latest news, but mostly it was the various village meetings he was called upon to advertise.

An outstanding personality in Wymeswold and a much-loved one
was a Mrs Goodburn, always called Sarann, which was short for
her full name of Sarah Ann. She did not mind her friends calling
her Sarann, but she bitterly resented new residents calling her by
this name. Once when our new young vicar called her Sarann, she
was very indignant and told him she had a handle to name and
would he mind using it, if you please?

This lady was left by her husband with two little children to bring
up. There was no Social Security then, but she gallantly set about
the job by taking in washing and going out charring, even cycling to
outlying farms a couple of miles away to earn just that little extra.
She always wore a big black hat trimmed with a huge red rose.
Sarann was such an honest person. I remember that when she
found a five pound note, she took it along to the police who said
that, if no one claimed it within three months, the money would be
hers. No one claimed it and Sarann became rich beyond her
dreams, as at that time she only earned one and sixpence per day
plus her dinner.

In our early farming years, cattle that needed taking into Loughborough or Melton Mowbray cattle markets had to walk – five
miles to Loughborough or eleven miles to Melton market. The
man in charge of the cattle, who was called a drover, was Charlie
Brooks. A few days before market day, anyone who had cattle to
send contacted the drover to arrange where the cattle were to
congregate. When it was the Melton Mowbray market, a very early
start was made for the eleven mile journey. Mr Brooks had to make
a time allowance in case any of the cattle broke loose from the main
herd. This happened mostly during extremely hot weather when
the gad fly or horse fly was busy, sending the cattle mad with
irritation. Suddenly one would start off, tail in the air. Immediately
the others would follow, making them uncontrollable, until the
whole herd became exhausted. We called this stampede 'gadding'.
The drover would ask young boys to help drive these herds into
market, paying them a matter of pennies, but lads loved this job, as
it took them out of the village into the towns, otherwise they would
never leave the village from one year's end to another. Farmers paid

the drover around one and sixpence for each animal. Pigs were transported in a horse-drawn vehicle, covered by a strong rope net to keep them in.

A gentleman named Mr Rennolds, who had retired from business as a tinsmith in Loughborough where he had lived for many years, came to Wymeswold, where he took over an outlying smallholding. I think he must surely have worked harder in his retirement years than when he ran his own business. His work was so good, nearly everyone in the village asked him to do jobs for them. He once made me an electric copper kettle. I was so proud to own a real copper kettle, standing it in the hearth and polishing it to a high degree. Unfortunately, it came to a sticky end. We were going for a week's holiday, so the night before we left I did everything possible in order to make an early start, even to the point of filling my kettle. Then, inadvertently, I switched it on. When Sid got up the next morning, he called: "Nell, come downstairs at once and look at your prized copper kettle." I rushed downstairs, wondering what on earth had happened. Oh dear! My lovely shiny brand-new kettle lay in a melted heap all over the hearth with the element lying in the middle. I was very upset, but Sid said: "Buck up Nell, it's no good crying over spilt milk and we are not letting this spoil our holiday, so get cracking." Spilt milk, I thought, more like melted copper. I pulled myself together and got cracking, rushing about getting breakfast and getting the children ready for the journey.

Perhaps the most colourful character was a woman named Emma, who lived in our village all her life. When she died, Wymeswold lost a beloved lady, who could say any mortal thing to anybody without giving offence. These are a few of her stories.

A gentleman named Captain Pepper lived part of his life next door to Emma, of whom he was extremely fond. He spent many hours with Emma and her husband George. On one particular day Captain Pepper began to feel unwanted, as Emma was throwing out remarks that made it abundantly clear that he was not welcome. Captain Pepper was loath to accept this brusque treatment from his lifelong friend, so he asked her straight out why he was not wanted. "Well," said Emma, "if you must know, I've got a lady a comin' to pee, and I want to get me house nice and tidy afore she arrives." This was the day the Quorn Hunt met in the village and this particular lady always called at Emma's house before mounting her horse. "Come, come," said Captain Pepper, turning very red, "I think I'd better be going." "Yes, yes," answered Emma, "I think you better had, as I ain't much time left to get meself shifted."

This second story is a bit harder to write and perhaps should not be repeated, but Emma told me this one herself so I know it to be true. Nobody can write it for other people's enjoyment like the way it was when I listened to Emma's droll way of telling it. Emma was talking to one of her friends who had a large family of children and was expecting another baby. "Emma," she pleaded, "what can I do? If my husband only hangs his trousers on the end of the bed, I'm pregnant again." "Well," says Emma with her particular kind of snort, "I'll tell you what I would do. I would get the carving knife, I would cut it clean off, and gi' it to the cat." She was the only person I ever knew who could say such atrocious things and get away with them without giving offence.

She was also a tremendous entertainer on the stage and was always given a part in our village plays, since she only had to be her natural self to be a huge success. She seldom stuck to her script and often made up her own words, which caused great merriment among the audience but was a nightmare for other players. Sometimes when she forgot her words, she would say to the audience: "I've forgot me words. You'll atta wait a minute while I look in me little book." By the time the audience had got over their laughter, Emma had looked in her little book and had put it back in her pocket, carrying on with a straight face just as if nothing untoward had happened.

Emma was a well-known figure at all the garden fetes and village socials, sitting with her bran tub full of small toys and tiny packets of sweets, with her Spinning Jenny board on a table beside her. "Come, my dears, a penny a spin," she cried. The children loved her and spent a large part of their money spinning away, hoping the point would stop at a prize, which it usually did. Dear Emma made sure of this, surreptitiously nudging it on a little to a prize stop. Emma could not bear the look of disappointment on a child's face. When we lost Emma and her George, Wymeswold people felt bereaved of someone who only comes their way once in a lifetime.

In the village we used to have a lot of gypsies who came begging and selling laces and pegs at back doors. One day the most handsome gypsy I ever saw came to our door. She had straight black hair with a fabulous complexion. She was dressed beautifully and was as clean as a new pin but she was definitely a gypsy. I refused to buy any of her wares, so she peered into our living kitchen where she saw the sides of bacon, including a pig's chawl, hanging from the ceiling. The chawl is the under-jaw of a pig, which is usually salted down along with the rest of the pig and hung from the ceiling to dry. The gypsy looked me staringly in the face and, pointing her finger at me, demanded that I give her the chawl. I looked just as straight at her and told her: "No, I will not give you the chawl." She was standing about one yard outside the door, I was about the same distance inside. Gradually she moved towards me, still pointing her finger and staring me in the eye, repeating over and over: "You are going to give me that chawl." I stood my ground, although by this time our noses were nearly touching. I said slowly and firmly: "*I will not give you that chawl.*" By this time she realized that she could not hypnotise me, for I was smiling sarcastically, I must admit. She furiously turned from me, shouting the most horrible curses upon me. None of these threats ever came true, but I often wondered how many chawls she might have obtained in this frightening manner, had she found a more timid person than I proved to be.

Not all gypsies are the same. Once we had a grand lot who asked to stay a few nights in one of our fields, while they went round the villages selling their wares. Sid liked this band of gypsies and agreed to their staying. When they left, they came to see how much they owed Sid for the rent, but he told them they were welcome. They insisted on leaving us several kinds of brushes which lasted for years.

The next character story happened many years after. It was during a very cold winter spell that another knock came at our door, just as we had sat down for tea. It was dark outside, the wind was howling and snow piling up into drifts. Sid answered the door and there stood the fattest tramp imaginable. Sid said to him: "Come in, man, out of the cold." He sidled in, along with a shower of snow flakes, and said he was cold and hungry. Sid gave him a cup of tea and a huge slice of bread and cheese which he ravenously ate, still standing just inside the door. Even at that distance he smelled horrible. He asked for several more things, including money, which Sid gave him, but when he asked for cigarettes and matches, Sid refused, as he had visions of the tramp lying against a stack of hay or in a barn and starting a fire.

However, at this moment, the tramp spotted one of our boys laughing. He thought the laughter was directed at him and became very angry, telling my sons he did not like them, but he liked the little girl sitting next to them and he would give her something. We all sat transfixed as he felt in his top coat pockets but found nothing. He took off his coat and felt into the pockets of a second coat, then a third. This went on until six coats lay on the kitchen floor. With the shedding of all this clothing, we could see the tramp was not fat at all; in fact, he was terribly thin. Eventually, from the pocket of his seventh coat, he brought out a parcel in wrapped newspaper. He slowly unwrapped it and there appeared a lovely pair of pure white, beautifully clean fur gloves. He leaned over the tea table and presented them to the little girl. We watched him fascinated as he slowly dressed. The smell from him and all his coats was terrible. When he asked for something else, Sid said in a firm voice: "Come on my lad, you have done very well, now you must be going." So off he went, armed with lots of newspaper to keep his feet warm.

3 FARM ACCIDENTS AND DISEASES

Accidents on the farm happened mostly with horses and sometimes they were quite frightening. I remember following a huge load of hay drawn by our young horse Blossom up a short, very steep hill called 'The Knob'. Although Blossom was exceedingly strong, the load was taxing her strength, but she was a horse that never gave in. During the struggle up that hill the harness broke, the weight of the load took the mare off her feet and gradually lifted her higher and higher. Sid raced to the shafts, putting all his weight into trying to keep the load down and to save Blossom from strangling. At the save time he shouted: "Nell, fetch the carving knife," which I did pronto. Being a fast runner in those days, I had the knife there within minutes. Both Sid and Blossom were becoming exhausted. He panted: "Cut through that strap just there, Nell." After a great effort on my part, for tackle was strong, I managed to cut it through, thereby releasing the horse from the cart. Blossom lay inert for some time and we were praying that she would recover. Sid was in a state of exhaustion – only a very strong man could have held that cart from strangling the horse as long as he did. I was not much better, but my stress was due to anxiety for both man and horse. We all recovered our equanimity and made arrangements for the load to be removed by another horse.

Our older mare, Daisy, was Blossom's mother, but she had a different temperament altogether. Blossom was easy-going but full of guts, whereas Daisy was flighty and would jib at a heavy load. When tackled to the cart, she had been known to run away at the slightest provocation. Once she ran out of control, racing a couple of miles downhill into the village. Sid heard the commotion and raced into the street just in time to grasp the reins, gradually bringing her to a stop. Not many men are brave enough to stop a runaway horse and cart – a man has to have strength and courage to try such a dangerous feat. But Sid said he thought of what might happen to little children playing in the road down in the village, so he did not hesitate. Streets were playgrounds in our young days.

One morning I was awakened by a persistent hammering, which was unusual and had an urgent sound as well. I dressed hurriedly and raced to the scene of the noise, where I found Sid trying to hammer the fastening out of the concrete which held a cow's chain. Sid could not undo the chain as it was much too tight, so the only chance was to force the chain away from the concrete. We were much afraid, as we had already lost a beast during one night in this position.

Deep dykes caused serious accidents when animals slipped into them. I remember one of my father's best young horses getting itself wedged in a dyke. We found it on its back with its legs in the air. We never knew how it got in that position or how long it had lain there, but it was far gone by the time it was man-handled out of that dyke, taking a long time to recover.

Sid and I had a beautiful young roan heifer which was very heavy in its milk yield. A few days after calving, she went down with milk fever. The vet gave her an injection of calcium but told us to keep an eye on her as she might need another dose. Sid happened to be out one Saturday evening, so I went to the field alone to see if she was alright. I found the calf but could not find the mother. After walking round the hedgerows, I discovered her on her back in a dyke. Now what to do? Suddenly I thought there would be men in the pub, only five minutes away if I ran very fast. I had never been in a pub before but I raced in, panting, saying: "Please could you help. We have a young heifer in the dyke and Sid is not at home." Without a word the men rushed up to our field and with such a weight of men lifting and pushing, the heifer was soon out of that dyke but she could not stand. She was once again down with milk fever. I rang the vet who was soon over on his motorbike. We gave the beast another injection of the calcium and within an hour she was on her feet again and feeding her baby. In our parents' young days, many beast died of this dreaded milk fever and it was always the heavy milkers that went down. Then it was found that it was a calcium deficiency that caused these sudden deaths in the newly-calved beast. Since calcium injections started to be used, very few deaths have occurred.

A thing every farmer dreaded with a milking herd was a cow slipping her calf. Only a farmer realized the terrific financial loss this trouble could cause, because it was catching to other in-calf cows and lessened the milk yield.

A cow that goes her full time will usually have a healthy calf plus a flush of milk up to eight gallons per day, but an animal that slips her calf half way through her pregnancy never produces half that quantity. Our herd suffered this complaint once during our farming life. Every morning when Sid entered the cowshed, he would look nervously around for the unmistakable sign of a miscarriage: blood in the gutter, soon to be followed by a dead calf. This contagious abortion is called brucellosis and, after it has been diagnosed, a great deal of disinfectant is used in an endeavour to stop the trouble spreading.

One of the things an honest farmer resents strongly is a dishonest farmer getting rid of his affected animal by sending it to market. To make it look healthy, the cow is not milked for a couple of days, which swells the udder and makes it look a good milker. Then, just before the cow leaves the farm, the hind parts of the beast are washed to hide the usual tell-tale signs. After we suffered this catastrophe, we rarely bought from a market an animal that had recently calved. We would buy from a farmer we knew, but mostly we reared from our own herd. Years before this time, my father had suffered many losses from brucellosis.

Another great worry to farmers was when foot and mouth disease was confirmed in any part of the country. Those unfortunate farmers whose stock was affected had to have every cloven-hoofed animal on their farms killed, burned and buried. The government paid compensation, but a farmer who had taken years to build up a herd of pure bred cattle or pigs, rarely recovered from such a blow, as it was impossible to calculate the long-term financial loss. A caring farmer not only loses financially, he loses his life's work and all the animals he has cared for over the many years. During a foot-and-mouth epidemic a standstill order goes out to all farmers within an area of many miles from the affected farm. Cattle markets are closed and a farmer has to obtain a permit to move any cattle for any purpose whatsoever. This means every animal can be traced if the need arises. This drastic procedure is the only way of wiping out this dreaded disease which is extremely expensive to both the government and the farmer, but this method has proved very successful in past years.

An accident that David will always remember happened when he was stone picking in a field that had recently had a pond cleaned out. The sludge out of the pond is spread over the field but there always seem to be a lot of stones mixed with it. David was filling the float with stones when one of its wheels came up against the sludge-bumper   the receptacle used in cleaning out the pond. The horse took fright and dashed away leaving behind the wheels which separated from the chassis. This frightened the horse more than ever, and he finished up by smashing the float to bits. He was caught with just the tackle on him. Fortunately, no one was hurt, but we had to buy a new float, the other one was a write-off.

Sid and Bob were splendid with horses and good at breaking in young ones. I remember well when they were asked to break in a pair of magnificent grey shires for a gentleman living in the next village. They were delighted to be trusted with this job and took special care with them, training them in the fields for a longer period than was usual. Sid and Bob were pleased with the progress the horses made, and at long last they decided they were ready for the road. They tackled them into the heavy carts, Sid taking the reins and leading the first one, then Bob the second. I stood watching from the farmhouse doorway. Everything went fine as they went down the yard, but just as they reached the gateway, a herd of young beast, just let out after being shut up all winter, galloped headlong into the way, just in front of Sid's horse, which took fright and started to gallop away. I could see that Sid was not going to hold it and shouted to Bob to go to his aid. This meant that Bob had to leave the other horse for me to hold, but he was much too strong for me. He reared and turned suddenly and galloped up the stack yard, breaking down a strong five-barred gate. This stopped him momentarily and enabled the owner of the cattle to catch and hold him securely.

I breathed a sigh of relief about that one but was terribly worried about the other horse on the road, in case they had not controlled it. Fortunately, with Bob's help, they held it in check and all was well that ended well. Sometimes when anything untoward happens like that with very young, partly-broken horses, it spoils them for a very long time. The only damage was the broken stackyard gate, but a new gate was nothing at the side of the damage a runaway horse could have caused on the lane. These two beautiful great grey shires were eventually fully broken in and their behaviour was something Sid and Bob were very proud to have had a hand in. The owner, Mr Derbyshire of Rempstone, was also delighted with them. We never heard if he learned of the episode that happened on the lane at the bottom of our yard with his two valuable animals.

This reminds me of a narrow escape one of our labourers had with a bull. He came back from an outlying field called 'The Goosenest'. where we kept a herd of young heifers running with the bull. This bull had never been known to turn nasty, but the young man came back frightened to death. "Please don't send me up there again," he pleaded. "That bull went for me, and I only just managed to dodge round the stack and jump the hedge, I was so frit." Sid said to him: "Such rubbish, Dick. He was only anxious to get at the hay you were giving the beast; it wasn't you he was getting at. Anyway, Dick, have you foddered the beast?" "No," answered Dick, "I dare not. He was so mad, stamping his feet and shaking his head. Please, I can't go again, I tell you I'm frit to death."

"Alright," said Sid, "come on, I'll go with you and show you the bull is not dangerous." It was not long before they were both back, cleared out of the field, escaping in the nick of time, with the raging monster of the usually quiet bull stamping after them. "I really don't know what we are going to do," said Sid. He was afraid of what could happen if anyone else ventured into the field, not knowing there was a bull going mad. All our friends and neighbours were always welcome to take a walk in all our fields. After a lengthy consultation with Bob, they decided to ask a number of men friends to help catch the bull, then put a strong chain in his nose which would impede the bull so much that most people would avoid being hurt. It was with feelings of trepidation that I watched this army of men armed with staffs and hay forks leave our farm in an endeavour to master the bull. They were joking all the way. To me they seemed excited and unafraid, even looking forward to the fight they knew was imminent. When they had gone, I was like a cat on hot bricks, I just couldn't settle to anything. When eventually they all came back, I breathed a sigh of relief as I counted the men back into the yard. All looked safe and well.

Sid explained to me how they had managed to subdue the bull. As soon as the men entered the field, the bull rushed at them. They scattered without harm coming to any of them. This happened a number of times, then, at a given word, all the men attacked the bull with their staffs and hay forks. The surprise element worked well. The bull fight was now in reverse: the men were chasing the bull, but not without a few more efforts on the part of the bull to try to beat them. They cornered the bull, two of the men grabbed his horns, and the chain was fixed into his nose ring. Sid said it was the sheer weight of the numbers that beat the bull, but he didn't half sulk as he watched the men go out of the field with their backs to him and he could not do a thing about it with a chain hanging from the ring in his nose.

That bull walked the rest of his life with a chain to contend with, but he never tried any of his antics again. In fact, as we learned afterwards, he was only protecting one of the young heifers that had come into service.

One spring we were rearing chicks in the way of that time – around one hundred chicks in a hut, using a paraffin heater in a contraption called a hoover, under which the chicks snuggled to keep warm. We had six of these huts standing on a hill in the orchard, which was not an ideal position, as they caught whatever wind there might be. For several days that spring we had winds of up to one hundred miles per hour. Although these huts were staked to the ground, the wind blew one over and it caught fire. I was on my own at the time, as the men were all away. I pumped two buckets of water and raced up to the orchard to pour water on the worst of the flames. Several more bucketsful were needed. I was lucky in seeing that hut go over, otherwise one hundred chicks would have burned to death. Afterwards I fell on to the grass breathless and exhausted, chiefly from fright, and the chicks got a severe wetting.

One year after we had finished rearing our chicks, I got to thinking these huts were only being used part-time, so I decided to buy some turkey poults and fatten them up for the Christmas trade. Against advice from more experienced people than myself, I bought thirty poults, and was given one extra making thirty-one. I had good fortune and reared all thirty-one until seven weeks before Christmas, when I noticed one turkey looking a bit sorry for itself. Its comb had turned black, and after a few days it stopped eating and died. To my distress the turkeys kept dying until I had less than half of their original number. They had died from the dreaded disease called Black Head, which is a liver complaint, at that time incurable, causing blackening of the comb.

I was really upset at losing these turkeys as I had worked very hard with them. They had caused me a lot of trouble during the late summer hot weather. The little blighters flew up into the trees instead of going into their hut, and I had to take a ladder and reach for them out of the branches. This was really hard work, because the turkeys weighed twelve pounds and more by that time, and left me with a very bad shoulder with pulled muscles which bothered me for many years. Although this flock of turkeys, in spite of the heavy losses, paid a good profit, I was never inclined to raise any more; they had caused me so much pain and suffering.

4 CON TRICKS

At one time there came a man to buy a flock of pullets from us. He seemed quite a nice, honest sort of man, paying cash for the birds, but asking if he could borrow our crates to take them home in. Sid readily agreed, not even asking for a deposit on the crates, but he did ask for the man's address which he wrote down on a piece of paper. The man promised to bring them back for us in a few days, but weeks went by without his returning them, so one Sunday night we took the family out in the car for a ride, thinking we could call at the address he had given us to remind him we needed the crates rather badly. We found there was no such address where he said he lived, and no one knew a man of his name, so we lost our brand-new crates which had cost us one pound each. Shortage of money made one very canny as regards both the spending and the saving of it, but one cannot win every time.

We were not quite so gullible when two men drew their car into the farmyard and asked if they could buy four cases of eggs which were in short supply at the time. Four cases contained one hundred and twenty dozen eggs. The men offered more than the going price, so Sid helped them load up the eggs but they said: "Would it be alright if we paid for the eggs when we come the next time?" Remembering the crate episode, Sid said: "No, it will not be alright. You pay for them now or you don't have them." The men either would not or could not pay, so Sid calmly unloaded the eggs and wished them good morning.

Honest people find it hard to believe the tricks some folk will play for their own gain. One confidence trick I remember well happened during our last few years at the farm, when two nice-looking young men with Canadian accents came to our door selling books. They were extremely clever in the way they set about persuading us to buy their different kinds of books. They told us that a neighbouring farmer's wife had ordered over thirty pounds worth. They said they were Canadians, which caught me on a soft spot with our son David by then living in Toronto, Canada. I wanted to treat these boys as I hoped David would be treated over there. I asked them inside and gave them a salmon tea with a nice crisp salad. We thoroughly enjoyed their company and gave them an order for fifteen pounds worth of books and paid for them. We even gave them David's address in Canada, hoping they would visit him. We signed a number of forms, they gave us a receipt, and we parted like old friends. They said the books would arrive in about three weeks. I never knew just what made me ask Sid that night if he thought those two boys were genuine. He said: "I'm sure they are. Whatever makes you think they are not?" I answered: "I have just had a funny feeling come over me that we have been conned and we shall never see them or their books ever again." Sid said: "Ring our neighbour who they said had ordered all those books." I rang her but she had not ordered any. My intuition was right: we never saw them again or received any books. I wrote to David in Canada giving him the address on our receipt. He made enquiries but there was no such firm and no such address in Toronto in the book trade.

A year or so later, another man came to our door, trying the same dodge. Sid told him to clear out of our village or he would inform the police just what he was doing, then he chased him out of the yard with the yard brush. We learned afterwards the police were on the trail of these con men. Indeed we never had any more trouble and never heard of anyone else having it.

While writing about con tricks, my mind goes back to one that could have proved disastrous for me. This story happened many years later when my children were grown up. A man knocked at my door and asked: "Could I tarmac the drive?" He quoted a very reasonable price, to which I agreed. He then asked if he could use my telephone to ring the firm who supplied him with the tarmac. I heard his side of the conversation which to me did not ring quite true. I also noticed how very interested he seemed to be in one or two really nice pieces of antique furniture that I had in the hall. He then asked me to pay for the job before it was done, but I remembered an old saying of my father's: "There are only two bad payers, one who pays before he receives the product, and one who never pays at all." So I refused. He then said: "Will you pay half for half of the work?" I answered: "No." Next he brought a rough-looking workman who said he had come to prepare the drive, but all he had was a spade. I asked where all his machines and tackle were, and he gave me a queer answer. I began to feel really worried. He said: "They will all probably be here tomorrow at nine o'clock." Then they both left.

That evening a garage owner rang me and asked me if I had given the order for my drive to be tarmacadamed. I told him I had, but I was beginning to have doubts as to the two men's integrity. "You are quite right to have these doubts, Mrs Smith," he said. "Listen while I tell you what happened today at my garage." The two men told him that they had contracted to tarmac my drive, and asked him if, while they were preparing this, he would service their van. This he agreed to do, and when they called back for the van, they also asked him to fill the tank with petrol. They then asked him to make out their bill, adding the cost of the petrol. While the proprietor was in the office making out the bill, they raced away, never intending to pay.

On the assumption that they would be coming to start our drive the following morning, we made detailed and clever plans to allow them up our drive, then cordon them in with a tractor and trailer. The garage man and two of my stalwart sons waited from before nine in the morning until near midday, but the men never turned up either on that day or since. I was lucky, but the poor garage owner lost the value of a day's work on the van, plus the spare parts, plus the petrol.

We also had a bad experience once with the eggs we sent to the Melton packing station. We suddenly started having a large number of second-quality eggs, for which we received only around one shilling per dozen. This went on for weeks, the number getting greater and greater, until out of around two hundred dozen eggs, eighty dozen were recorded as second quality. We began to suspect that there was something very wrong at the packing station end, as at that time I was using six eggs every morning in the frying pan and had never found one egg that was imperfect. I rang the manager and asked him if I might come over and see our eggs graded, because if they were as bad as he said, then we would have to find out the reason and rectify it.

We made an appointment but, not trusting this manager, I asked two other farmers' wives who were having the same trouble to go with us and to take along forty dozen more eggs just in case. We arrived at the appointed time and were shown about twenty saucers with an egg broken into each one. They looked awful: the yolks were a kind of purple colour I had never seen before in my life and have not since. We were not the only dissatisfied farmers at that meeting. It was market day and the numbers kept growing. The manager gave us a talk as to what was wrong with the eggs, and I never heard such rubbish in all my life. When the manager had finished talking, I said: "May I ask a few questions?" "Oh yes," he said, "fire away." And my, didn't I fire away! I asked him why I had never seen an egg yolk that colour, though I always broke six every morning for our breakfast, and why did all our seconds get to the packing station. I told him he had talked a load of rubbish to very experienced poultry keepers who did not believe a word he had said. Then I asked the other farmers if they had ever seen an egg yolk that colour. They all shouted "No, not" By this time some of the farmers were getting quite angry.

I then asked if we could all go to the grading room to see my week's eggs graded. "Sorry," said the manager, "your eggs have all been graded and have been sold." That was after we had made the appointment to see them graded! "Never mind," I said in a sweet kind of voice, "we anticipated some thing like this would happen, so we farmers' wives have brought forty dozen more eggs." He

could not refuse, so we fetched in the eggs and we all trooped into the grading room. Out of all those forty dozen eggs, he picked only one tray of thirty eggs that he said were of second quality. Not one of us could see any difference under the light, so I asked him to explain just what was wrong. "Oh," he said, "they won't keep." He was just going to bring down the stamper of the little lion, when I got hold of his hand and stopped him. Then I dropped my biggest bombshell. I told him: "I do not want those thirty eggs marking with the little lion stamp." The little lion was stamped on eggs sold in those days to prove that they were laid in England. I told the manager that I had a food inspector from Leicester at the meeting and he was going to test the thirty eggs every week until they started to go bad. I never saw a man so deflated.

A woman aged about sixty sat next to me. She had not said a word at the meeting, but she told me afterwards that the previous week she had had eighty-one dozen eggs graded as second quality out of just over one hundred dozen. "But, my gell, how you told him straight! You said it all for us. I wish I could talk like you did, gell." This woman's husband was in bed after suffering a heart attack. She had been up that morning milking the cows at four o'clock to enable her to come to this meeting. Even so, she had missed her bus and had walked many miles because she was so worried about her eggs. I was so glad of what I had said and done, if only for her sake.

The food inspector came to our farm every week to test the eggs the manager had said would not keep. After eight weeks he said he was not coming round again, as they would never go bad. From then on I used one every day; they were perfect until I used the last two. The whites of these two ran a little but were used in a cake. I sent the inspector's report on these eggs to the packing-station with a reminder of what had been taking place. After some research it was found that the manager had been invoicing eggs as seconds and then had been selling them as perfects, pocketing the difference in money, which was considerable. Needless to say, he quite rightly got the sack, but he was not charged, so he was quite free to do the same thing again at another packing station. Some town people think people in the country are dull and nothing exciting ever happens there. How wrong they are!

One day a gypsy man walked into our farmyard saying he had a pony for sale, and would Sid like to buy it cheap. We did not really want a light pony like that, but she was so lovely and so dainty, I could not resist her, so Sid bought her and called her 'Gypsy'. She had the energy of the young and teased our heavy horses mercilessly. She would creep up behind them, then bite their behinds, turning like lightning and galloping away. One day she did not escape so easily. A huge shire we named Harby turned just as quickly and gave her a terrific kick in the groin. This caused the pony to walk very lame indeed, so we sent for the vet who diagnosed a split stifle. He held out little hope for her recovery, but we were fortunate, for with treatment she completely recovered, with only a scar to show for what had happened. This scar took off quite a lot of value from the pony. After breaking her in, we sold her for quite a good profit and she made a wonderful child's pony. Years later the thought came into my head: "Where did the gypsy get that beautiful pony? I hope he didn't steal it."

5 ANIMALS

There is always something interesting happening on a farm, especially with animals, like when our dog Judy had pups at the same time as our cat had kittens. Judy had her pups inside a building on one side of the farmyard, the cat had her kittens on the other side. When Judy's pups were sold, she stealthily crept across the yard every time the cat left her kittens and carried them over to her puppies' bed. The cat in turn watched for her chance, and every time Judy left the kittens, she took each one by the scruff of their necks back to their own bed. The children loved to watch this backwards-and-forwards business that went on until the kittens were all given away.

We had two cows who in their own way were an absolute phenomenon. One learned to open the gate that opened into the stack yard from the fields where the cows grazed. But how in the wide world did she know when it was milking time? I expect by her full udder of milk. Sometimes when Sid was late home, this cow opened the gate and all the cows would troop down the stack yard and into the farmyard and wait to be milked. I often had the doubtful pleasure of tying them up.

The other cow learned how to turn the handle of the pulper which cut up the mangolds and turnips. She would stand and lift the handle up to the top with her nose, and then bring it down with her chin, thus cutting the food. She would eat every scrap the machine had cut, then start all over again.

A farmer's wife was expected to do many unusual kinds of work. I remember one exceedingly wet summer, when the hay harvest had been long and wearisome, and many acres were spoilt, blackened by the continual rain. The harvest was just as bad: the ground was sodden and the binder had great difficulty in moving. Our two horses, Daisy and Blossom, were weakened by an attack of worms, no doubt another catastrophe caused by the wet ground. They got stuck time after time, so Sid came back to the house and asked me if I would ride our thick-set, very strong pony, to help the two weakened heavy horses. We called this pony 'Roger the Dodger' – he was right lazy, and I knew that the one who rode him that day would need a whip. Sid helped me on to this fat pony, whose back felt like a table top between my knees. I was riding first horse for over six hours, at the end of which I was so stiff I just could not dismount. I called to Sid: "I need help, I can't get off." He did not believe me and just laughed. I was much too proud to plead for help and had another try. I did not make it but fell off, luckily into Sid's arms. For two days I was so stiff I could hardly walk, but I was comforted by the thought that, through my help, a field of wheat was stooked, waiting for the sun to dry it. That year the sun was reluctant to shine and one farmer named Mr Burrows was carting his last field of corn in December.

Another hard job came my way when Sid was ill. My son Sidney and I went to shut up the six hundred hens that were on free range. That day we had endured a terrific snowstorm, a blizzard was still raging and it was bitterly cold. Before leaving the house, I built up a huge log fire, placing another heap of logs by Sid's side, telling him to make sure to keep the fire going as the logs burned low. We dressed in our warmest clothes with scarves and gloves and set off at a brisk rate, but the snow was so deep we were very soon slowing down to a walk. We shut down the slides over the little entrances the hens used to get into their huts and had only one more to close, this hut being the farthest away. To our dismay, someone had put down the slide during the day and had shut out all the hens which then had crept underneath the hut. There was only one thing to do: young Sidney would have to creep under the hut and pass the hens to me. The dark hour came long before we had finished this task. We knew that, if any hens were left, Reynard Fox would kill them. Sidney was exhausted and stiff with cold, I was not a deal better, but we trudged home, looking forward to a good fire and a hot drink. Sidney was crying with the hot aches. We left our outdoor

36

clothes in the kitchen and thankfully opened the sitting room door. What did we find? Sid immersed in an interesting book and the fire completely out. I sat down on the rug and cried with cold and disappointment. Sid was even more upset than we were. He offered to relight the fire, but I refused to let him, chiefly because lighting fires was not one of Sid's strong points and we needed a fire as quickly as possible. Young Sidney has never forgotten that traumatic scramble across the snow-covered fields and coming home and finding the fire out.

One year we raised a lot of our bull calves. The vet castrated all of them, and when they were old enough, they were turned out to grass. Sid wondered if he was doing right, as his father always maintained that raising bullocks for meat was only a gentleman's pastime, but that year the calves were making hardly anything at all. In fact, calves were taken to Melton market and were not sold, so a farmer had to bring them home again. During that time, it was not unknown for a farmer to find a strange calf in his trailer, deposited there just to get rid of it. Our bullocks did remarkably well, even though their last winter had been a hard one. We did make quite a fair profit on them, but we made a mistake in selling them all for the Christmas market. We learned afterwards that we should have sold half of them one year and the other half the next year. We had a great amount of income tax to pay, because the profit was counted on the one financial year. We live and learn: we were very young and had paid little tax until then.

In the countryside farmers have a lot of trouble with dogs worrying the sheep. This happens mostly when dogs get together in a playful mood in a field where sheep are grazing. Their play frightens the sheep, making them run away from the dogs. The dogs love this, thinking what a lovely game to play, but their play turns wrong when they taste blood, which gives them the desire to kill. Some dogs can be cured of this. Many ways are tried, some of which are successful, but the odd rogue dog is never cured and has to be put down. Often a farmer will shoot a dog, if he sees it worrying his sheep. He can do this within the law, but only when the dog is seen actually killing the sheep.

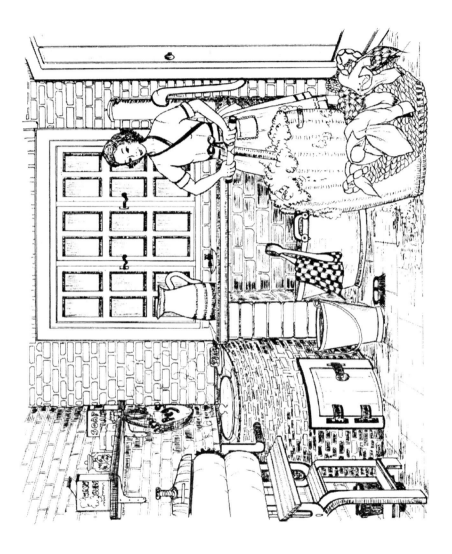

The same thing used to happen with hens on free range, but this seldom occurs these days, because most hens are safely housed in battery houses and never have to face this awful slaughter. In the old days we lost many birds through killer dogs, for which we never received any compensation.

Once, when one of our own dogs became a killer of hens, the cure we tried was wholly successful. One of the hens it had killed was tied with a chain around the dog's neck. It hated this, but the hen was kept in place for several days, until the dog was heartily sick to death of dragging it around. It never killed another hen.

One of the best cures for a sheep-killer dog is to shut it up for a while with a ram. At first the dog is full of fight, but he soon finds a ram a very different proposition from a ewe. He does not run away, he fights back, ferociously butting the dog with his head. The dog soon tires of this treatment and becomes frightened. If a dog kills a sheep after this treatment, nothing will cure him.

We once had a beautiful pure-bred black labrador by the name of Sam who thought it great fun when a flock of sheep came into the home field. We were so afraid that the fun would turn to worrying when we were not around, but when the ram was brought in for the mating season, the tables were turned. Sam made the mistake of playing with the new ram who turned on him and gave him a hard butt. Sam, still thinking this was play-acting which hurt, had another go and was knocked flying. This taught him to behave, a lesson he badly needed, and being a sensible dog, he gave in graciously. After this, he was trusted with the sheep.

Children can also cause havoc on farms. During the early part of the war, when evacuees were sent into the country, we saw a nine-year old boy wander into our farmyard and into the orchard, where we were raising around five hundred chicks. This boy killed many of them and just left them lying on the ground. Then he attacked my washing which was hanging lovely and clean on the line. He covered it with blood from the chickens and muck from the ground, then he tied pyjama legs and shirt sleeves to the sheets, and any other garment he could see he tied into knots. When I found this slaughter and all my week's washing ruined, I could have wept. The boy's parents were sent for. At first they just could not believe their son could have done such a dreadful thing. They offered to pay for the damage, saying they would have to take him home, bombs or no bombs. After I got over the shock of a boy that age perpetrating such a horrific deed, I wondered if he had done it because he was unhappy away from his parents and wanted to make his parents fetch him home. If that was so, it certainly worked.

The next story is most amusing, even though it cost us a whole day's eggs from around six hundred hens on free range. A three-year old nephew of ours wandered into the fields, where there were around ten huts which housed all our laying hens. He crept into the huts through the slide where the hens went in and out. Only a very small child could manage to do this. He carried a stone with him and then systematically broke every egg in every hut.

His father questioned him about this, but the child absolutely refuted the idea that he had been in the field. His father believed him, but I had seen him walk into the yard and up into the fields. I used a bit of guile the next time he came to play with my children. I walked out into the yard with a bar of chocolate in my hand. I called out: "Who wants to share a chocolate bar with me?" Of course, all the children cried: "Me, me, me." So I chose young John, asking him to take a walk with me into the fields where, while he was enjoying his chocolate, I said: "Which hut did you break the eggs in first?" "Oh, Auntie," he said, "I did dat one first," and then he pointed to a hut, "den dat one, and den I did all the others!"

I then said: "Didn't Mr Conscience tell you you were being very naughty?" "No, he didn't Auntie. Who's him?" he asked. I explained that he was a little man inside him who told him, without speaking, when he was doing something very naughty. The answer I got was: "Ooer, Auntie, it's a good job that little Mr Conscience man wears a big hat, or I should have drowned him this morning when I drank two full cups of tea!" What could a woman say to answer that one?

During the early years at the farm, Sid, Bob and a number of their friends used to go rabbiting on Sunday morning. They started out with their dogs, ferrets and spades, keeping to our own land. When they did not have much luck, they started to trespass on a neighbour's land. Some neighbours did not mind, so long as they were given a fair share of the rabbits, but others hated these young men taking their rabbits and warned them off their land. They still persisted, so that in the end they were run off and had to leave one of the spades behind.

When Sid arrived home and disclosed the happenings of the morning, I was cross and told him they were poachers and quite in the wrong, and that I was not in the least sorry that they had lost their rabbits and one new spade. The excitement of this Sunday morning poaching really got hold of them. They stopped out for longer and longer periods of time, which meant the lovely Sunday dinner became later and later. I got so tired of overcooked meat and washing up late in the afternoon, that I told Sid dinner was at twelve thirty every Sunday, and if he was not there, his would be served along with the rest and would be allowed to get cold if he did not arrive. He said: "You wouldn't do that, Nell." I answered: "Yes I will", and I did. Sid was quite shaken when he returned home and found his dinner a congealed mass and his cold batter pudding on a side plate. I told him I worked hard all the week helping in every way I could, that I deserved a few hours of rest on Sunday afternoon, and that he was the cause of this being denied to me. He had never thought of it in that way and was very sorry. He was never late again, although he had to stand quite a bit of ribbing from his poacher friends.

A few years later this sport came to a halt. A disease called myxomatosis attacked rabbits all over England; they were dying like flies. The only time I saw one suffering from this disease was when a boy caught what he thought was a big rabbit. "Oh dear! I said, "child, you have picked up a rabbit with myxomatosis." I called Sid: "Do come and put this poor rabbit out of its misery." It looked awful, its body was swollen to a huge size, and its eyes which stood out were already glazed. Sid killed this pitiful object, then they both buried it. Because of this disease, nobody would eat rabbit and it was years before one was seen on our farmland.

Another thing Sid and young Bob loved doing together was mole catching. They became quite professional mole catchers, using proper traps in their runs. They skinned the moles, then stretched the skin tight, tacking it on a board to dry. When the required number was reached, the moleskins were sent off by post to be made into coats, which were very fashionable at that time. Sid and Bob received sixpence for each skin, but when moleskin coats went out of fashion, that was the end of their mole catching. They did not really mind, as the moles were becoming fewer and much harder to find, but we did miss the little bit of extra money. The land suffered less from those destructive mole-heaps all over the fields, but I could never get over feeling sorry for those lovely inoffensive little animals.

6 CAR ESCAPADES

Sid had many escapades with his various cars. I remember once we left our Ford Consul in the forecourt of a garage to have a new handle on one of the doors. We both went our different ways, arranging to meet at the garage later on. I arrived first, obtained the car keys, paid the bill, then started to walk to meet Sid whom I met driving a Consul out of the garage forecourt. I asked him where he had got the car keys from, and he answered: "They were in the car." He would not believe me when I told him that was not our car, so I asked him to look on the bench front seat, which, on our car, had a mark. Of course, it was not there. Then I waved our car keys at him and pointed to where ours was parked. He said he felt awful, sliding this car into the space where he had taken it from.

Another episode happened in snowy weather. Sid, my brother John and I took young Sidney to Loughborough to see a film called *Jessie James*, starring Tyrone Power. Because it was freezing so hard, Sid left the car under cover, inside the forecourt of a garage that we traded with. We all enjoyed the film immensely, but when we came out of the cinema, there was a thick fog, and we could only see a few yards ahead of us. We groped our way towards our parked car, thanking God we had left it under cover and it would not need defrosting. But when we got there, oh dear, we were aghast to find our car gone.

We thought it must have been stolen, so we went to the police station to report the loss. They suggested that, as we had left the car where we were known, the garage owners might have taken it inside, as in those days very few people locked their car doors. The policeman rang the owners who confirmed that this was what had happened. However, they absolutely refused to make the journey to

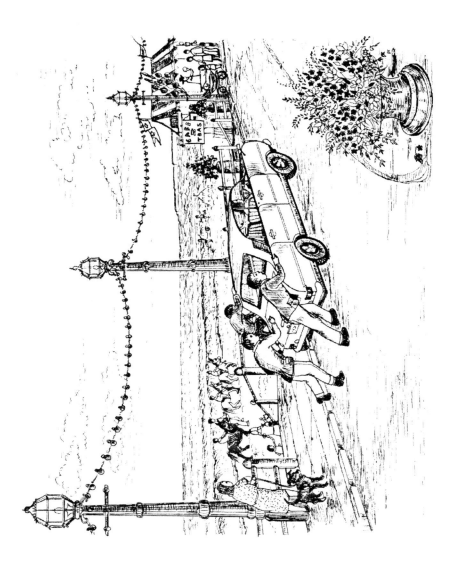

the garage on such a dreadful night at the hour of ten-thirty at night to release our car.

The police suggested we take a taxi, if we could get one to drive out to our village in the awful fog. They rang and persuaded a driver to try but that was all he could do: try. When we found ourselves broadside across the road with the bonnet of the taxi a few inches from the side of a factory, the driver declared he dared not go any further. We were also worried about him getting home on his own, so we saw him turned round safely and then we started the five-mile walk home to Wymeswold. About a mile and a half out of Loughborough, we walked out of the thick wall of fog into a beautiful clear moonlit night. Had it not been for carrying Sidney most of the way, we would have enjoyed that bitterly cold moonlit night's walk. Sid, John and I carried him in turns and when we reached the village, we were glad for John to take him in to sleep with our mother, as Sid and I had to walk the length of the village to our farm.

Another time Sid had parked our very first brand-new car, an Austin Ten, in a street in Melton Mowbray while he did a bit of shopping. On his return he placed his parcels on the bonnet, while he tried to unlock the driving-seat door, which he failed to accomplish. Now Sid, who had the utmost patience with all animals, had no patience whatsoever with anything mechanical that would not go right straight away. He had started to fume and use force, when a heavy hand clapped him on the shoulder and a voice said: "What are you doing trying to get into my car?" Sid turned furiously round and said: "What d'you think I'm doing? I'm trying to get into my car and the key won't open it." The other gentleman asked Sid the number of his car. Sid told him, then looked down at the number of the car he was trying to get into, and was aghast to see it was not his own car's number. The gentleman then pointed to a car a few yards away. "Is that your car, sir?" Of course it was, and Sid made a very deep apology.

A laughably funny incident happened when we went on a holiday to Skegness. We parked our car in front of the hotel on the promenade where it stayed until the next week when we were ready to go home again. This was allowed a few years ago. The battery had become flat and the car would not start, so I was asked to drive while Sid and a couple of friends pushed. They pushed for quite a while for about a quarter of a mile along the prom, until they were out of breath. One friend gasped: "Sid, you get in and drive. Nell will never start it." Sid got into the driving seat and I took his place, pushing at the back. Within a few yards the car started and I got in to find Sid helpless with laughter. He said: "Nell, you chump, you never turned the ignition on!"

All these years after, I still chuckle to myself when I visualise Sid and our friends pushing that big car all the way along the prom. One shouted: "Nell, have you got the brake on?" They never thought to shout: "Have you got the ignition on?"

On our way home we stopped to buy some food at a little shop. We were still giggling so much the assistant said: "What's the joke?" When we told her, she too went into hysterical laughter. The other girls wanted to hear about it and we left the shop with that happy noise ringing in our ears.

When I first learned to drive a car, I did not realize that an experienced driver could drive any car, so I was greatly embarrassed the first time I took ours to the garage to be serviced. The mechanic said: "Leave it in the forecourt and I will move it inside when we are ready for it." I, fool-like, said: "Can you drive a strange car? Would you like me to show the gears to you?" He looked at me so pityingly, I realized the bloomer I had made. I was such a novice. Talk about 'Fools rush in where angels fear to tread.'

One day, when Sid was driving into Nottingham, the police stopped him for speeding in a built-up area. Silly-like, he made the excuse his speedometer was not working properly. "Oh," said the policeman, "that is the second offence." The result was a fine and Sid had to appear at the Nottingham court. Just for the experience of watching a court case, I went with him. He was fined the usual amount, but both of us had found listening to the other cases interesting.

We did not realize that while we were both away in Nottingham, young Bob had caused another court case which had to be held at Loughborough. Sid had set Bob, as his work for the day, to go onto common land where we had permission to cut some stakes and binders in readiness for a hedge they were cutting. Bob left the common land and entered a spinney, which he thought was an extension of the common land and where the stakes and binders were so much better and far easier to cut. He had a good load when a farmer drew up and asked him: "Just what are you doing, young Smith?" "You can see what I am doing," said Bob in a belligerent kind of manner, "I'm cutting stakes and binders for hedge cutting." "Well", answered the farmer, "you get yourself out of there, as you have no right." "Oh, yes I have," replied Bob, "my brother Sid has got permission." One thing led to another, until Bob and the farmer were near to fighting and tempers were flaring. All this ended in the farmer fetching the police, and Bob was brought to court for trespassing and cutting stakes and binders without permission.

This was how Sid and I spent another whole morning in another court listening to other cases until Bob's case came on. The case was dismissed and the farmer who brought the case apologized to Sid, saying he was so mad at young Bob's cheek that he had reported him in a temper. He then said: "We have always been good friends, Sid. Will you shake hands and let us forget the matter?", which of course Sid did.

I was much amused at the man who was reporting the morning's cases. He came up to us and asked us if we would explain to him just what stakes and binders were for. He said: "I have never in all my life been so puzzled as how to write up this case. What with cutting stakes and binders and using them for hedge-cutting, I am completely bewildered." "Ah," we thought, "townies don't know the first thing about country life." Sid explained things to him quite simply and the reporter seemed quite satisfied to obtain an unusual story for his paper.

We had several bullocks in an outlying field and, as the winter was a very hard one, I remember Sid said it needed two people, as the car kept getting stuck in the snow and he wanted me to drive while he pushed. At one time we needed to go twice a day to this outlying field, the furthest from the farmyard. One day we had to drive through snow a foot deep and, to make matters worse, a terrific blizzard was blowing. The fast-falling snow was all over the windscreen and no tracks had been made on the lane, which made it more difficult. Sid was driving and I was leaning out through the open window saying: "A little more to the right" or " A little more to the left" or "For God's sake, stop, Sid, we are nearly in the dyke!" or "We are on the grass now; I'm sure we have left the road." We managed to travel a mile and a half, unload the hay, and carry it over about twenty yards of grass verge to the hungry bullocks.

Now came the worst job of all, turning the car round in the road. I drove while Sid pushed, but time after time we had to dig ourselves out of the deep snow, placing sacks under the wheels to get a grip. After superhuman efforts we got the car turned round. Sid shouted: "Keep her going Nell, while I gather up the sack and spade." These he threw into the car boot, for if we stopped the car, we would have the digging to do all over again. Sid clambered into the car and we were away again. The final relief when we arrived safely home was indescribable. Still I felt content when Sid said: "Thanks, Nell, you're a pal. Those beast would have gone hungry, if you had decided not to come." The weather plays such a big part in farming, more, I should say, than in any other business, except perhaps the fishing industry.

One day during a very busy time on the farm, Sid asked me if I could possibly take a yearling calf to the Leicester abattoir in a trailer behind a car. I took a friend with me, thinking we might have a little shopping spree afterwards. Everything went well until I stupidly drove the wrong way down a one-way street. People kept gesticulating and pointing to the signs. "O lor!" I thought, "you've made a bloomer, Nell. How are you going to turn round in this narrow street with a trailer behind, complete with calf?" Just then a policeman strode up to us. I thought: "Now for it, Nell", and I said:

"I'm so sorry, I didn't know this street had been made into a one-way street. I'm a country lass, but I should have known better." The policeman said: "Never mind, me duck, I'm a country lad myself. I'll help you turn round." He stopped traffic while he unhitched the trailer and I turned the car round, then he fastened the trailer back on to the car and directed us to the right road for the abattoir. I was very grateful: things could have ended so differently, another policeman might have fined me. We reached the abattoir safely, unloaded the calf, parked the car, then started our promised shopping spree.

After a time we were looking at fur coats and I noticed a lovely brown musquash, just the coat I would have loved to own. My friend said: "Let's go in and you can try it on. One is not bound to buy it." I tried on the coat and it fitted perfectly. I said I would love it but could not spend all that money without my husband's permission. The owner of the shop said he would save the coat for me until the next day, to give me time to talk with my husband.

When I got safely home and told Sid that evening all about our adventure and all about the coat, he said: "I will take you into Leicester tomorrow and have a look at this fur coat you like so much." I worried about the price, saying that forty-two guineas was too much to spend on one coat. I thought of so many other things that amount of money would buy. I was much moved when my two little boys came up to me saying: "Close your eyes, Mummy, and hold out your hand." Into my hand the eldest boy, Sidney, put two pennies. Then the five-year old David slipped in his twopence alongside. Sidney, thinking he, as the oldest, should give more than his kid brother, gave me his last twopence pocket money. After a short hesitation David brought out his last penny saying: "Open your eyes now, Mummy." In great surprise I counted, and with tears in my eyes I hugged them for the lovely present they had given me.

I put these seven pennies in a special part of my handbag and we set off for Leicester where Sid saw me try on the coat. He just quietly said to the shopkeeper: "Will you accept a cheque?" We had no cheque cards in those days. The shopkeeper said he did not usually accept cheques for that large amount from strangers but from us he would. I then brought my boys' gift of seven pennies out from their special place and told him the story. Sid made out the cheque for the coat, less the seven pence, and in this way the boys would always know that their seven pennies actually helped to pay for their Mummy's brand-new fur coat. I still wear that same coat forty years afterwards and it is practically as good as new.

7 WE LOSE A FRIEND AND FIND ANOTHER

It was before the start of the war that Miss Simpson, whom we always called Aunt Becky, became seriously ill with cancer. She had been a family friend since long before I could remember. She kept the shop in Clay Street and managed it entirely on her own, apart from the odd few days when I would help her out, while she visited her sister in Wisbech.

I loved keeping shop, not only because it enabled Aunt Becky to have a few days holiday, but because she had been so good to me through my teenage years and early married life, when money was so short. During those years she had great influence in my life, guiding me through difficult periods, especially when I left work as an apprentice dressmaker and, with only a few pounds, started a business on my own in a room she had prepared for me above her shop. She was an experienced dressmaker herself, and her advice was very helpful in building up a successful and good-class business.

When we had our first child she became a second grandmother to him, giving him more presents than most children received in those days. Until the day she died, she always bought his shoes. In fact after her death we found shoes in boxes marked with his name to fit him for many years to come.

I remember that, when she was ill with phlebitis in her leg, Sidney was the one who had to carry the hot bread poultice which had to be applied to her leg. I can still see in my mind's eye this little three-year old boy carefully carrying this poultice placed on a warm plate across the room to where Auntie Becky was lying on a sofa holding out her arms ready to receive it. She loved David, but no child was thought so much of as young Siddy as she called him.

When she became ill, it was obvious that she would have to give up the shop, so for a start we had a sale, reducing everything drastically. This took many weeks before all the foodstuffs were sold. She then became so ill we had to close down, and shortly after the war began, we took her to stay with her sister.

During our stay in Wisbech, we all spent a day at Sandringham. On the way there, we made a stop where we noticed a most beautiful garden. When we reached Sandringham, the children asked for an ice cream. I looked around the car for my handbag, and to my dismay I could not find it. My worst trouble was the fact that I had all the brand new ration books in the bag. Whatever would we do without them?

This loss spoiled my day at Sandringham, but I had one great hope: that when we had made the stop on the way, near that beautiful garden, I might just have dropped my bag on the grass verge. We were with our host and he wanted to go home another way, but I was adamant we were going back just the same way we came, just in case. Our host told me I was mad, as it was a million to one chance that on a Bank Holiday Monday I would find my handbag. We slowed down our car on nearing the place where we thought we had stopped. I called at the house nearest the spot and asked the owners if they had seen a handbag lying on the grass verge anywhere near there. "Why, yes," said the lady, "it lies about two hundred yards down the road. It has been there all day, along with a gentleman's trilby hat and a pair of gloves." I breathed a sigh of relief. I had forgotten that I had nursed Sid's hat along with my gloves. I thanked the lady very much, then she said: "I think the reason they were not picked up was because only a few yards away a young couple had been canoodling in a small hollow and they had been there nearly all day too. I thought the bag belonged to them." We clambered into the car, travelled that small distance, and there to my delight lay my handbag, along with Sid's hat and my gloves and, best of all, my ration books. Our host, who in the beginning had been quite cross because we took that million to one chance, was also delighted for us.

I have been extremely lucky on two other occasions when I have carelessly lost my handbag. Once I left my handbag on the bonnet of my car when I parked it in a garage. Luckily it was still there when I returned. The other time was when I left it on a counter in a shop where we were buying furniture with money which had been given to us for a wedding-present. I nearly collapsed with relief when I found that bag sitting on another counter in another part of the shop.

Eventually Auntie Becky came home to Wymeswold and her condition gradually became much worse and she needed constant nursing. I was spending most of the day with her and my sister Lottie helped with the night nursing. During this time Sid's mother helped at the farm and gave my family their meals. We sent word to her sister telling her how ill Auntie Becky had become and she came as soon as she could, but after a few days Auntie fell into a coma and died. I remember her last words to me before she died: "Goodbye, my good kind friend." But there, I have never had a better friend than she had been to me.

Her house, goods and chattels were put up for auction, and her house, garden and orchard were sold during that first year of the Second World War and realised £350. Since then, the property has changed hands several times, each buyer making improvements until, at the last auction, the new buyer gave over £20,000 for it. I expect if the property came up for sale today, it would easily fetch over £30,000 or even £40,000. Old houses in good repair seem to make more money than the newer type of house in Wymeswold.

When Sid and I decided we could at last afford a holiday, his father was surprisingly against the idea. He said he had been married for years and years before he had a holiday, and that farmers, even in our days, could not leave the farm so easily. In the end he and Bob promised to look after everything for us, so off we went for a week to Skegness. Besides our family we also had my sister Lottie with us. I looked forward to the rest, as the last holiday I had had was on our honeymoon and the only other holiday had been when I was eighteen years old. Unfortunately, the holiday ended with young Sidney being taken ill with enteritis. I always thought he caught this through the unclean house in which we stayed. I strongly suspected that the sheets had already been slept in. As we had gone to Skegness 'on spec', this was the only place we could find that had a vacancy sign displayed and no wonder. We had the doctor to Sidney when we got home, but it was many months before he began to pick up. It was many years before we managed another holiday.

It was during a later holiday in Skegness that we met an old man called Clem Lofthouse, who put right the discomfort I had long suffered in my right shoulder. We were all staying in the same house as a lady who was afflicted with a stiff arm, caused by a fall two months previously. She said she could not hold anything in her hand and one finger stuck out and would not bend. One day Mr Lofthouse said to this lady: "Come and sit outside. I can put your arm and hand right." The lady gave him a pitying kind of look saying: "I have been under the best of doctors who have told me nothing can be done for it." He persuaded her to sit on the garden seat while he manipulated her arm, and within half an hour she was back inside waving her arm up and down and round and round and moving all her fingers. The next day I plucked up my courage and told him about my very bad shoulder, which had stopped me playing tennis and also impeded my everyday work. That dear man manipulated my shoulder around for half an hour, then said: "Get your racquet. You will be able to play tennis now." And I did, and never had that trouble again. We became great friends and over the years realized the relief from pain countless people enjoyed as a result of his ministrations.

One could write a book on the stories he told. One summer he spent a week with us and I told him he had to make this one week a real holiday and not do any manipulations. But no, he couldn't, and having no humans to work on, he started on our animals. He noticed one of our cows was walking very lame, so when the chance came, he surreptitiously started to manipulate that huge back leg. Afterwards he came into the farmhouse 'all of muck sweat', as country people say, and really out of breath. "Good gracious," I exclaimed, "whatever have you been doing?" "Aw," he answered, "that owd black cow will walk a lot better when you turn her out after milking." She sure did.

One day he stood watching Sid milking a newly-calved heifer who had a lump at the back of her udder the size of a golf ball. "Caaw," said Mr Lofthouse, "I'll soon manipulate that lump away. Is the old begger quiet, Sid? I don't want to be kicked into that muck." Sid assured him she was a docile animal and did not kick, so he started very gently to manipulate the udder around the lump. The animal loved it. I think she would have stood all day enjoying that udder being rubbed. After about half an hour of this treatment, Mr Lofthouse said: "She'll be alraight now", and the lump had disappeared.

He told us about a man who went to him wearing a huge collar around his neck, asking him if he could help, as he had been under many doctors and specialists without any improvement to his condition. With those clever fingers he worked on this gentleman for over an hour, calling the doctors names and using all manner of swear words about them all the time he was working. When he had finished, he said to the man: "You can have your cards now, man, and don't put that bloody contraption on your neck again." "Ohl" said the gentleman, "won't I need to come again?" "Not unless you want to," said old Clem. "Well, I do want," said the gentleman. The second time he visited Clem, he told him he was a specialist doing intricate operations, until the trouble with his neck stopped him working altogether. "Aw," said old Clem, "you should've told me you were a doctor yoursen, I wouldn't've swore and called doctors to you like I did." That doctor was soon back at work helping people back to health as Mr Lofthouse had helped him.

Sid, like other farmers doing work that needed great strength, pulled muscles from time to time, and then it was to old Clem he went and without fail came home much better from Clem's manipulations.

People who owned greyhounds used to take their animals to Clem the day they were due to race. He would work all over their bodies, then say to their owners: "The bugger'll win now!" And quite often they did. Old Clem used to swear in nearly ever sentence, but I loved that dear old man.

8 THE SAD STORY OF
LITTLE JOHNNY

The first time I made contact with little Johnny's family was when his mother came to our farmhouse door to ask if we could supply her family with their daily milk. She was a delicate-looking woman in her late thirties. We agreed to sell her the milk but, after a few weeks, the family began to get into debt and owed more and more for their milk. Sometimes two and sixpence was paid off the ever-increasing debt of pounds. I tried to encourage the mother to pay her way but the milk debt grew larger and larger. Sid and I discussed the matter and Sid decided in his usual generous way, to allow the family one pint of milk per day, instead of the usual order of two pints. We knew full well we would never see any return, as we realized that her husband was not giving her enough money to pay for food and milk. However, the thought of her children was uppermost in our minds. There were three children in the family: two girls and a lovely little boy named Johnny, who was born with a handicap. He had one good arm, but his other arm finished at the elbow, which had a wee thumb on the end. He overcame this handicap in ingenious ways, managing to do many things with the aid of this little thumb. The mother was heavily pregnant and looked dreadfully ill.

One bitter cold morning, just before Christmas, the children all trooped into our warm kitchen just as we had finished our breakfast. They walked round the table, their eyes searching the left-over food. It was with dismay that we realized for the first time we were looking at abject hunger on three little faces. I asked the children what they had eaten for their breakfast. "We haven't had any breakfast," they cried, "not today, not yesterday, and we had no dinner yesterday either. Mummy is poorly and cannot do any work." I looked at my well-fed little boys who had just eaten a couple of rounds of beans and toast, then I looked at Sid who gently nodded. Understanding Sid's nod, I asked the three children if they would like some beans on toast. "Please, please," they cried. I opened another large tin of beans and set about toasting the bread. Poor kiddies, they cleared up every crumb, then they returned to their home with the milk. To my surprise, they turned up again while we were having our midday dinner. I invited them into the kitchen, out of the cold, then asked them what they had come for, but could not get a word out of them. Once again the children walked round the table; one knew they were hoping for another meal. That day, I had made huge rice pudding, more than enough for one meal, but we liked to eat the remainder cold for supper. Instead, the hungry little children ate it all up.

I spoke to our postmistress, Miss Joy Brown, about their hunger problem, and we decided that Joy should give the children their dinner on most days of the week, and on her busy days I would give them their dinner and each morning their breakfast. Joy and I made up a Christmas parcel for them and Sid sent round a rabbit for their Christmas dinner.

This state of affairs continued into the first week of the New Year, when our district nurse knocked urgently on our door, appealing for help. Apparently the children's mother was in the last stages of labour, she had no fire and no bed, only an old sofa, no blankets and nothing whatsoever prepared for the coming baby, only one new nappy and an old clean shirt. The nurse had asked to go upstairs where she had found a double bed, in which the whole family slept together, covered by old coats. The three children were still in bed. The nurse said: "Please help me Mrs Smith", then rushed back to her patient, saying it was too late to get the poor woman into hospital. I set about doing what preparations I could. Sid hopped on his bicycle and went to ask his mother to help as well, then he shovelled some coal into a sack and brought it to the children's house where a neighbour lit a fire. I searched through the baby things I had kept and also brought downstairs a spare mattress which we scarcely ever used. All these things were placed around the fire to air. Sid fetched downstairs an old iron single bedstead, loaded all these things into the float and took them to the poor woman's house. Meanwhile the nurse had delivered another baby boy, who unfortunately was born with a deformed club foot. He was bathed and dressed and placed in a long drawer which served as his cot. The bed was made up for the mother who had been delivered on the old sofa.

The nurse was greatly worried about the other children, who were still upstairs in bed and had had nothing to eat all day. Temporary shelter was found for the two girls and Sid and I took little Johnny home with us. The poor little lad was in such a state, Sid and I just did not know where to start, for he must have slept in his jersey and knickers for several nights. His pants were full, the stench was dreadful. I asked him how he had come to be in such a mess. He told us that, having only one hand, he could not undo his bracers and his mother had been too ill to help. We spread thicknesses of newspaper on the floor in front of a good fire. I used scissors to cut away as much of his pants as I could, then sat him in a warm bath to soak off the rest. We burnt his clothing outside and, after he had been given a lengthy soaking, we used a long-handled soft brush to ease off the worst of the hardened excrement. This was done three times in fresh warm water, then we bathed him properly.

By this time it was eleven o'clock, but while we had been at work, Sid's mother had been busy also. She had collected from her friends a complete layette for the new baby and clothes, including a lovely dressing gown for the mother for when she was about again. The next morning I went to visit the mother who was being looked after by a neighbour. I took some nourishing broth made from boiling some beef. I found her so weak that she could not sit up to take the broth, so I asked her husband to get the doctor. "The nuss will soon be here," he replied, but his wife was so ill I begged him to do as I asked. I lifted the mother up in my arms and fed her the broth. She fell back, gasping her thanks. I covered her up and went to look at the baby who had not murmured while I helped the mother. I was shocked to see the baby was dead. I told the poor mother. She said she knew her baby had died, but she had fed it. "I really have fed it," she kept repeating. I realized she had not even the strength to lift her baby, and in any case a baby does not die in a few hours because of lack of food. I waited with her until the arrival of the doctor and nurse, who did everything that was necessary. The verdict at the inquest on the baby was that it had died from natural causes. The mother who looked yellow became gradually worse, and on January 8th she died of cancer of the liver. I remember the date so well, because it was my birthday and we were having a family party when we heard the sad news. I told little Johnny he had lost his Mummy because she was so ill, but the poor child had been living with us for a couple of weeks and was quite happy and content. He seemed not to worry at all.

Johnny spent the next six weeks with us. He used to help me pack the eggs into their boxes. He loved doing this until one day, when he dropped an egg, he became dreadfully upset, surprising me by going into hysterics and taking a long time to be calmed down. "Aren't you going to hit me, Mitiff Miff?" he cried. Johnny could not pronounce my name and always called me Mitiff Miff, which sounded so sweet from his little lips.

After about three weeks, his father came to see him. Johnny became hysterical again, hiding behind my skirts and crying: "Mitiff Miff, don't hit me, Mitiff Miff, don't hit me ever!" This last outburst made us all wonder what this beautiful child had suffered at the hands of his brutal father. Sid and I discussed the possibility of adopting this motherless child. We had two grand boys of our own and they too were quite happy to welcome him into our family, loving him as we did, but this was not to be. Johnny's father came again to tell us that his sister was going to bring Johnny up. My heart sank: this aunt had a very large family of her own and her husband was a farm labourer earning less than two pounds per week. Although this lady would do her best, I knew Johnny's life would be very different. Instead of growing up in our spacious farmhouse, being well fed and clothed, he would be living in an overcrowded cottage, sharing the food they were able to supply. My heart ached to see him taken away. He wore a little check coat that my sister-in-law Sybil had given him, and he looked very smart but oh so very sad. He had been so excited when he had been given clothes to wear and toys to play with. While living with us, he told everyone who came to the house: "I sleep in a tickle white bed all to myself." He could not get over having a bed all to himself.

It was quite some time before we saw any of Johnny's family, until one day his aunt came to tell me that Johnny was in the Loughborough Hospital, dying from the last stages of consumption. Unfortunately, at that time, I was confined to bed with a torn bladder, owing to an accident on the farm. The doctor had ordered me to stay in bed for at least five days to allow the wound to heal and to stop the bleeding. Therefore, I was unable to travel to the hospital to see little Johnny. His aunt came once again with a message from the matron of the hospital, asking once again if I could please go and see Johnny, as he was delirious and kept calling for Mitiff Miff. He was also going through the motions of packing eggs in their boxes, his favourite pastime while living with us. I left my bed on the fifth day, hoping to be able to make the journey to the hospital, but the bleeding started again and I had to wait another three days. To my great sorrow, it was too late by then to see that dear child again.

He was brought to his aunt's house in Wymeswold, where I went to see him. They had dressed him in a pair of our son David's blue pyjamas, and he looked so peaceful. I asked his father when the funeral would take place. His answer was: "I don't know. Nowt has been arranged, and I ain't got no money to pay for owt." This was certainly a problem for those who loved Johnny and did not want him to have a pauper's funeral. We solved the dilemma with the aid of his schoolteacher, Miss Florence Smith, who cleaned and polished her car and put the tiny coffin on the boot, that let down at the back. The four little bearers travelled with him. I took the chief mourners in our car to the cemetery, the rest walked behind. This sad episode brought to an end my association with Johnny's family.

One sister was adopted by an airman and his wife, stationed at Wymeswold. She had a wonderful home with loving parents. The other little sister was adopted by a farmer and his wife, living in the neighbouring village of Prestwold, and she too had an extremely good home and parents. The father remarried and had another large family, but he left the village.

It is almost too hard to believe that these sad events could happen is such a friendly village as Wymeswold, but the family had kept their troubles to themselves too long.

9 CHRISTMAS AND APRIL FOOL'S DAY

Right through my childhood days, Christmas was always something extra special, much more so than our birthdays. Mother used to say that, with seven children, birthdays came so often, she could not possibly give a party each time. Every Christmas, however, she always made it a party time, and when we started our own family, I tried to do the same.

We usually killed a pig a couple of weeks before Christmas, so there was always an abundance of food, never mind how many visitors we had: porkpies, sausages, faggots, haslet, fries and lovely joints of pork. Only once in a while did we ever buy a turkey. Christmas puddings were also made and boiled in the copper, just as many as it would hold, which enabled us to have a pudding on most birthdays and anniversaries as well. Mince pies and a rich iced cake were added luxuries.

We were never too busy on the farm at Christmas time, so we were able to enjoy everything along with our children. That was until Sid took it into his head to buy around sixty day-old chicks. These cockerel chicks were caponized, making them grow into huge birds which were ready for killing by Christmas. Sid plucked them and I had to draw out their insides. This was called dressing the birds ready for the oven, but to my way of thinking it seemed more like undressing them. I disliked this job and, after completing around fifty, I was absolutely tired to death of the hard work of pulling and tugging, and the mess that needed clearing up afterwards was really awful. Nowadays we have an electric plucking machine that does the job in a few minutes, and we sell the birds plucked but not dressed, apart from a few we do for our own freezer. These caponized cockerels paid very well indeed, making an excellent price for Christmas. This extra money was nice to have, but of all the dirty farm jobs I did, this was the one I disliked the most.

In spite of this extra hard work, we still managed to enjoy our usual happy times during Christmas. The children invited a number of their friends to a party, where we all enjoyed the same old games my family played when I was a child. These games seem out of fashion, now that television is in nearly every home and all these expensive remote-control toys are popular.

Yet sometimes I wonder if children today are missing something. Only a few days ago, I had two of my youngest grandchildren for an afternoon, along with one of their friends. They brought with them a number of their expensive Christmas presents with which they played for about half an hour. When I asked them if they would like a game of Ludo, they said they had never heard of it. I fetched out my forty-year old Ludo board, a few tiddlywinks and a dice. They helped me set out the board in readiness for the four players, and I taught them how to play this old-fashioned game. Within minutes those children were enthralled, first by throwing the dice and having to wait for a six before they could start a move, then by sending each other home and having to start all over again. They were so disappointed when they had to stop play because their mother had come to take them home. I was delighted to realize that these old games still held as great a fascination for today's children as they had in my young days, but I wondered how many parents would think to buy a new Ludo or snakes and ladders or even a game of Halma or draughts. After seeing how these six to eight-year-olds enjoyed it, I shall not hesitate in future to interest them in a few more old games that at the moment are buried deep behind other lumber.

Our family's favourite card game, which we always played at Christmas time, was called 'County cards'. We only ever heard of this game once outside our own house, yet that set is now at least seventy years old and, although it is dirty and many of the cards are held together with sticky tape, the fourth generation in our family still love to play this card game. The cards represent fifteen counties, with the names of two or more towns belonging to each county. There must be three or more players to play this game, and the winner is the one who wins the most sets of counties. County cards taught us kids more about the towns of England and which county they are in, than all our geography lessons put together. From time to time various members of our family have tried unsuccessfully to buy this card game. My sister Edna even wrote to the card manufacturers but they could not help, so Edna bought the required number of plain cards on which she painstakingly printed the exact counties and their towns.

Other games our children played which seem to have been forgotten are 'Hunt the slipper', 'I can spy with my little eye something beginning with' – the letter of the article that has been chosen. 'Oranges and lemons – the bells of St. Clement's', 'In and out the windows', 'Pussy come and sit on my knee', 'Blind man's buff', 'Postman's knock', and 'Brother I'm bobbed' were extremely good. I wish someone could write a book on all these games, how they were played and the tunes they were sung to, so that future generations could learn a little of how their forebears enjoyed themselves without the aid of the wireless, television and toys costing up to one hundred pounds or more.

The money things cost reminds me of the time we bought a clock. We had not been able to afford a real clock; all we had was a small alarm, given to us as a present, which we carried upstairs at night. When we saw that a shop in Loughborough called Latimers had a sale, due to the owner's retirement, we decided to go and look for a clock. I learned from my brother Warner that they were auctioning their clocks and jewellery off each evening. Warner said he had bought a real beauty for fifty shillings and they had one left which would be auctioned that night.

Having an eye for a bargain and really needing a clock, I raced up the field to Sid to see if we could go to the sale that night to try to buy the only remaining clock. To my chagrin Sid said: "No, we can't afford one just now, Nell." I turned and went back home, shedding a few tears which I tried to hide. At that time I had no dressmaking money in the kitty and I was far too proud to beg and pray Sid, but when he came home at milking time, he came into the house saying: "Get someone to look after the children, Nell, and put your glad rags on, we are going to Loughborough after tea." Sid had noticed my disappointment and had changed his mind about the clock. I gave him a prolonged hug and he pulled away saying: "We have to get cracking, Nell, if we are going to catch the bus in time for that sale." I was very excited, rushing around getting a babysitter, setting the tea table, putting on my best clothes and laying Sid's on the bed to save time. We caught the bus and bought the clock, bringing it home on Sid's knee on the bus, which caused quite a stir among the other passengers, as it was a wall clock measuring nearly a yard in length and around a foot wide. Knowing nearly everyone on the bus, we did not mind their teasing one little bit. We were in such a happy frame of mind at securing such a fine clock for fifty-two shillings and sixpence, and we still had not got over the excitement of the bidding.

Sid was a great one for a bit of fun, which often lightened our hearts during those war years. On April 1st he was in his element. Never did any of us escape being made an April fool.

We had recently acquired a new neighbour on the opposite side of the lane, an extremely nice old lady named Mrs Williams. Sid went to the village telephone box and phoned me, saying he was Mrs Williams's nephew. He asked me if I would be so kind as to go across to Mrs Williams's house and look to see if she had left her key in her front door, as she could not find it anywhere. I knew Mrs Williams had gone to visit her daughter, so I ran across the road and looked in both front and back doors. I found no key, so then I searched the ground but still no sign of a key. I raced back to the phone full of apologies. There was a strange quietness over the phone. I began to fear that I had taken so long the nephew had got tired of waiting. "Hullo! Hullo!" I cried, then came across the line the unmistakable chuckle I knew so well and I realized I had been made an April fool again. To disguise his voice, Sid had pressed on each side of his nose.

Another phone trick was played on a school inspector named Miss Hogg, who stayed with us for a few nights each week while inspecting schools in our area of Leicestershire. Sid thought very hard before playing an April fool's trick on Miss Hogg, but he just could not resist a chance. She was still in bed when he knocked on her door, saying she was wanted urgently on the telephone. Sid had lifted the receiver and leaving the door open just a little, he sat drinking a cup of tea, quietly listening. Miss Hogg was getting quite agitated saying: "Hello, hello," then again: "Hello, hello, Darcy Hogg speaking." After a while she opened the door, asking Sid if the caller had given a name. Sid replied with a straight face: "No, Miss Hogg, but it is April the first." The serious Miss Hogg was helpless with laughter and certainly enjoyed the joke.

Sid also loved to tease our dog Judy who was a one-man dog, following him wherever she could. If Sid ever left the yard without her, Judy would not leave the place until he returned. I remember once when Sid entered the yard, he had pulled his cap over his face, turned his coat inside out, bent himself nearly double and, shuffling his feet, slouched into the yard and up the path towards poor Judy, who was sitting on the mat outside the back-door. Judy was furious at this strange-looking object making growling noises, so she was determined to make short work of it and see it off the place. With her scruff up and snarling like mad, she raced down the path, but when she got to within a yard of Sid, he simply said: "Hullo, Judy." That dog stopped right in her tracks and my, didn't she show how sorry she was that she had not recognised her beloved master. She just jumped all over him, her excitement knew no bounds. As I watched this through the window, I thought to myself what a lovely man Sid was and how lucky I was to be his wife.

At one time we had a young boy named Benny Bennett, who worked on our farm. One April 1st Sid ran out of the house holding a large milk can. He thrust the can into Benny's hands crying urgently: "Make haste, Benny, run and fetch me a can of fresh air from the paper shop." Poor lad, he did not stop to think, he just rushed off to the village shop, pushing the can into the hands of Mr

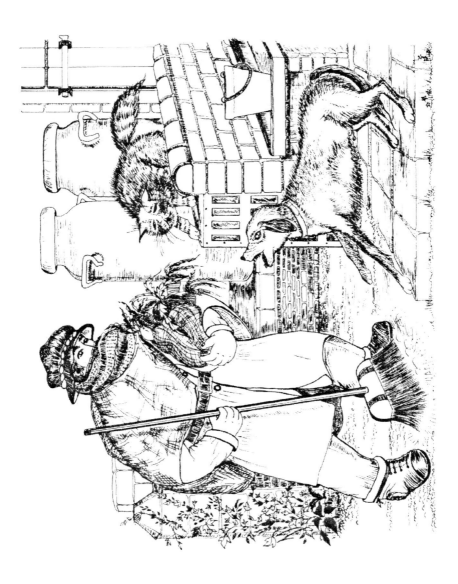

Thorpe the shopkeeper saying: "Be quick, Mr Smith wants a can of fresh air." Mr Thorpe was quick on the uptake. Pushing the can back into Benny's hands, he shouted: "Tell Mr Smith I have not got any in stock, but be quick, Mr Smith will have to send you somewhere else, but hurry, hurry!" Benny ran back into our kitchen, breathlessly gasping out: "Mr Thorpe is out of it, where else can I go?" Benny's face was a picture when Sid quietly told him it was fresh air he had been sent for and he was an April fool. He said Sid had sounded so urgent, he had not stopped to think, he had just run.

Michael was caught when Sid called him out of bed early, saying that Mr Jalland, the farmer, wanted help, as there were a lot of stray beast in his field. Michael hurriedly dressed and raced up the Wysall Lane, but did not find Mr Jalland or any stray animals. "April fool, Michael," laughed his father.

Once my brother Bill borrowed our farm trailer to fetch home a load of logs he had sawn to help out with the coal ration. When he came into our house, he was a bit worried about leaving a trailer full of logs outside all night. Sid said he was quite sure it would be alright, who on earth would want to steal his logs: Bill said: "You never know, I'm still a bit worried, there are some queer folk around." Sid persuaded him they would be alright. After Bill and Phyll, who were living with us at the time, had gone to bed, Sid crept quietly outside and removed a barrow-load of logs, hiding them where Bill would not immediately see them. In the morning when he examined his load of logs, Bill saw they were short and came fuming into the kitchen where we were having breakfast. He was shouting: "Someone has pinched some of my logs and I have a good idea who it might be. There are one or two sly folk about." Then he started naming names, so Sid had to confess to the prank he had played.

10   SECOND WORLD WAR

When the Second World War was declared, farming altered drastically in various ways. During the twenties and thirties farming was very unprofitable, and not enough money was made to plough back into the land. Men were laid off, and they and their families lived on the bare necessities of life. I knew one farm labourer who had five young boys and they lived on little besides bread and lard. The mother went out charring and took in washing. The poor of today are rich at the side of people out of work in my young days. During the war the government needed the farmers badly and, by paying much better prices, made it worth their while to produce as much food as possible. We were told what to grow. Wheat, barley and sugar beet were first on the list, and much more grassland was ordered to be ploughed up.

Everyone who could kept a few hens and, where possible, a pig. These were fed mostly on scraps saved by neighbours and friends. Potato peelings were boiled for both pigs and poultry. We used to sing a ditty about this practice:

> Dearly beloved brethren, don't you think it's a sin,
> When you peel potatoes, to throw away the skin,
> For skins feed the pigs and the pigs feed you?
> Dearly beloved brethren, don't you think it's true?

There was also a story about one labourer who asked one of his mates what he took into the field for his dinner. The man answered: "Well, I tecks two thick slices of bread, wi' a thin slice a bread in between, and that mecks a rate good sandwich, don't you think?"

When clothing coupons were made necessary, all sorts of economies were made. When the bed sheets were getting thin, we used to turn the sides to the middle to make them last longer. Mother used to say: "One must do this when the middle begins to wear thin, as if they are allowed to wear into holes, it is much too late to make a good job of the repair." We even made sheets out of calico flour bags, four unpicked flour bags making a double sheet. We also used to get flour bags made of thick linen, which were used to make table cloths and which were spoken for by our friends, even before they arrived on the farm. I saw some beautiful hand-embroidered tablecloths made with these bags. When a larger tablecloth was needed, a wide edging was faggot stitched all round the edge. I still have one of those cloths, which I do not use, because I would like to save it for my descendants, so they can see the kind of thing that was used and worked so beautifully during those long wartime evenings. Bags that were damaged were mostly used as tea towels. Nowadays all meal or flour is sent to the farms in paper sacks.

When America entered the war and Americans were sent over to England, we were very grateful for their help, but some things that happened with them offended our sense of fair play. I had heard that our own men, when having a night out, could not get served in many of our pubs. I just could not believe this, until one evening when Sid and I were on our way home after a long journey, we thought we would call at a pub for a drink and a bite to eat. We watched American airmen come and go, being served with the utmost deference and promptitude, while we and several other English people remained unattended. We sat there waiting our turn which never came, so after an hour and a half we walked out more hungry than ever. Apparently the Americans tipped so heavily that our servicemen could not compete. Happily not all publicans served our men so shabbily.

During the Battle of Britain, when our fighter planes were bringing down German planes, we invited a schoolmaster friend of ours to spend a weekend on our farm. It proved a long weekend, for he stayed for three weeks, working hard helping with the harvest. During every breakfast time Tivvy, as we called him, and Sid used to make small bets as to how many planes would be brought down on that day. I thought this was awful because each plane shot down meant someone's son being killed, whether it be a German or a British plane.

Some years later, when our men folk and a number of friends were gathering in a field of hay, an aeroplane, which had run out of fuel, crashed in the next field. Had it flown another hundred yards or so, it would have hit the stack they were making. The only man who saw it coming was driving a horse and rake towards it. The rest of them saw and heard just a large explosion. A red-hot rotor from the plane hurtled across the field towards the men, crossed a couple of hedges, and finished in the field behind the haystack, over two hundred yards from the plane. Some of the men rushed to quiet the horses, others went to see if they could help the pilot to safety, but sadly he was dead. Sid had to attend the inquest on this poor boy. The dreadful thing was that the plane was in perfect order, but had run out of fuel. A mistake had been made during the refuelling, as the plane had not travelled the miles it should.

Sid's cousin, Jack Moss, who lived with us for several years, was killed, or rather was reported 'missing, believed killed', while on a reconnaissance expedition in extremely bad weather, flying over the Skagerrak, a strait of water lying between Denmark and Norway. The plane with all its crew never returned. Jack was so young to die, but so many did during that awful war.

During the war we shared our large farmhouse with many servicemen and their wives and children. We made friendships with them that have lasted over the years. Our favourites were the Whiteley family from Morecambe. Arnold and Winnie and their two children lived with us for six months, six extremely happy months, until Arnold was sent to Iran and the rest of the family went back home to Morecambe. After the war was over, we spent many holidays with each other and we still correspond.

Another favourite couple was Viv and Eileen Moss with their two-year old son Peter. Viv became keen on gardening, so we allocated him part of our garden, where he grew many of their own

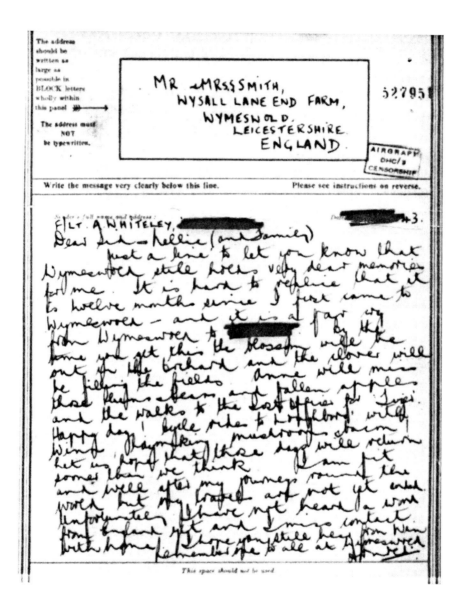

MR & MRS SMITH,
WYSALL LANE END FARM,
WYMESWOLD,
LEICESTERSHIRE.
ENGLAND.

52795

AIRGRAPH
DHC/9
CENSORSHIP

Write the message very clearly below this line.   Please see instructions on reverse.

F/Lt. A. WHITELEY,

Dear Jid — Nellie (and family)
        Just a line to let you know that
Wymeswold still holds very dear memories
for me. It is hard to realise that it
is twelve months since I first came to
Wymeswold — and it is a far cry
from Wymeswold to ...
time you get this the blossom will be
out in the orchard and the clover will
be filling the fields. Anne will miss
those plums above and fallen apples
and the walks to the Post Office for fags!
Happy days! Cycle ride to Loughboro' with
Winnie, blackberrying, mushrooming, etc.
Let us hope that those days will return
sooner than we think. I am fit
and well after my journeys round the
world, but my travels are not yet ended
unfortunately. I have not heard a word
from England yet and I miss contact
with home. Are you still here? New
Remember me to all at ...

This space should not be used

vegetables. At the same time we had a family living in a caravan in the home paddock. The husband, too, was mad on gardening and had turned over quite a large part of the field which we had fenced to keep out the animals. There was great friendly rivalry between these two amateur gardeners. I loved to sit in our living-kitchen with the door wide open, listening to their conversations about whose peas and beans were the best and who had grown the biggest potatoes. Nearly forty years afterwards we still enjoy the odd surprise visit from many of these people.

After the war our caravan was let to students from Loughborough College. John and Barbara Woodrow were very special. I remember so well the day they came. They had just been married and come straight up to Wymeswold from Lowestoft to spend their honeymoon in our caravan. I shall never forget the trauma of that day. I had let the caravan to a Nottingham lady and her daughter for six weeks on the condition they left a day or two before these two honeymooners arrived. Well, they would not leave, saying they had nowhere to go. They locked the door and would not open it to talk to me about leaving. I expected John and Barbara around four to six o'clock and these two were still locked in the caravan. I went up and told them I was fetching the police, as the new tenants were here and needed to be let in. I was dreadfully worried as to what state the caravan would be in when they did leave, but all's well that ends well – with the threat of the police, they left, and everywhere was clean and tidy. I invited John and Barbara to spend their first night in our spare room, but they said they were anxious to settle into their new home.

John was a marvellous actor, being a great asset at our farmhouse parties. He would turn his coat inside out, place one of Sid's old farm caps back to front on his head, pick up a walking stick and do an amusing impression of an old Norfolk labourer. Best of all, he imitated a constipated old lady who took her knitting to the toilet. The grunts and groans were really hilarious, with a shock ending of "Thank God for that" and "Ain't my knitting growed." Our sides ached with laughter, and when he said: "Now I will do the old

Norfolk labourer at the toilet with the diarrhoea", we all pleaded: "Please no more, we cannot stand any more, it hurts too much." Nevertheless, he did it and we hurt more and more with laughing.

Then I had my bit of fun, which turned sour on me. John had previously told me he could not eat raw onions, so I made an onion sandwich and placed it carefully on the top of the plate of other sandwiches. Thank my lucky stars he was so excited he picked the top one without even looking and took a deep bite. Oh dear, his face went almost green, he raced outside and was violently sick. When he came back, he was really mad, and told me off without mincing words. Didn't I feel small. I apologised profusely, but he was a long time forgiving me.

John's father was mayor of Lowestoft twice, with a school named after him – 'The Woodrow Comprehensive School'. Our family spent a week's holiday with John's parents in their splendid hotel at Lowestoft.

11 MY CHILDREN GROWING UP

It was during the war, in November, when David was nine years old, that he was taken ill with a mystery illness that was never diagnosed. We were so worried about him, we called the doctor in the early hours one morning. The doctor said he was completely puzzled by the symptoms, but as David was so dreadfully ill, he must be taken into the Nottingham Children's Hospital at once. Now at this time I was seven months pregnant with my third baby. Nevertheless, I prepared David for that awful journey that I knew we had to face. I warmed a huge woollen blanket, and wrapped it warmly around his wasted little body, then Sid carried him to the car, placing him on my knee.

It was one of those November nights of freezing fog, making the journey twice as long as it would have been under normal conditions. I was worried about so many things besides David's high temperature: would the awful journey kill him, would we arrive at the hospital safely, would the German bombers be over Nottingham again? Sid, bless him, was trying to comfort me, without any hope of really doing so. Then, to cap it all, a policeman stopped us in Nottingham to ask us what we were doing in the town at that time of night. I begged him: "Please allow me to close the window. My child is desperately ill, and my husband and I have to take him to the children's hospital." That policeman was wonderful: he told us the nearest way to the hospital, wished us luck, and said how sorry he was to have had to stop us, but it was something that he had to do during the wartime years.

David was isolated and kept in the hospital right up to Christmas and after. Then I begged so hard for him to be allowed home, they said: "Yes, but we still do not know what is the matter with your son." David had been home a few weeks when my third baby was born, so as he had been so ill, he went to live with his Grandma Smith for a little while. The second day he was there, David came out all yellow and we always thought he had been suffering with suppressed jaundice. Sidney and David had started to be ill at the same time, but Sidney's skin came out yellow at the start, and he got better quickly. David, with exactly the same symptoms, gradually became desperately ill, but when he turned yellow, all those weeks afterwards, his recovery was both quick and sure.

I was now able to enjoy my new baby, relieved of the anxiety of the previous three months. It was a boy, he was born on a Sunday morning, and we named him Michael William, always calling him Michael. I wanted to call him Richard, but my sister-in-law Kathleen said: "If I have a baby boy, I want to name him Richard." "Oh," I said, "alright, Kathie, I'll name this one Michael", a name which has suited him very well indeed. I had longed for this third baby to be a girl, but Michael was so beautiful that, after seeing him for the first time, I never once wanted him different.

Sid's Aunt Nan, who had come to live in Wymeswold after having her London house bombed, really spoiled baby Michael. She used to pop in to see us nearly every night, and nursed him until he was put to bed. The baby loved this petting so much that, when he was put down, he got into the habit of crying, and then Aunt Nan would pick him up again. This got so bad that, when he was put to bed, he raised the roof, screaming away. Aunt Nan would rush upstairs, pick him up out of his cot, and walk about the room with him until he went to sleep. The few nights Aunt Nan did not come, I had this same pantomime for hours on end.

Now when parents worked as hard as we did, much as we loved our children, we needed a few hours of peace and quiet. Sid was getting quite cross about this matter, so I decided to do something about it, something that was very hard to achieve. I asked Aunt Nan to stay away for one week, to enable the baby to forget this continual picking up every time he cried. "Oh no," she cried, "please don't ask me to stay away. I love the baby so much, he has helped me get over the bombing of my London home." I insisted, in the kindest

way I could, that the baby must not be picked up out of his cot, once he had been put down for the night. I told her she was spoiling him and that Sid was getting cross about it. After much persuasion, she agreed to stay away for just the one week, while we got him back to his usual routine, but after five nights she said: "Nellie, I have just had to come, I couldn't stay away any longer. I promise not to pick up the baby after he has been put to bed." Fortunately, the five nights had proved sufficient to break the crying habit, and Aunt Nan said she realized she had been wrong and that she had spoiled the child. How she loved the baby Michael! Sometimes, as he grew up, I felt quite jealous of his devotion to his Aunt Nan. Of course, she never chastised him, which I had to when needed. This, I think, was one of the reasons that he seemed to love her so much.

I remember with great sadness that, when Aunt Nan was dying, she would not allow the ambulance to take her to the hospital until we had fetched Michael out of school. She kept saying: "I won't go until I have said goodbye to my little tad." Michael could not sound an "l" and always called himself a 'tittle tad'. The nickname of Tad followed him all through his school days and long afterwards. Michael never saw his beloved Aunt Nan again – she died in Melton Mowbray hospital in a matter of days – but he has never forgotten the love and devotion she gave him.

By this time our eldest son Sidney, with the help of his Aunt Kath, had worked hard at his studies. He took his eleven-plus exam at school which he passed, and was admitted to Loughborough Grammar School. School work was not Sidney's favourite occupation, but he was always a very determined character, and whatever he tried to do, he did well. Farming was his first love and nothing ever changed him. His grit and tenacity, with hard work and a lot of luck, paid dividends, for now at the time of writing, he has bought a farm in Herefordshire with first-class land and a beautiful Georgian house.

David was just as determined in a different way. He loved schoolwork and wanted to be a schoolmaster. Again, with the help of Aunt Kath, he also passed his eleven-plus. David was ten when he passed the exam and he too travelled with Sidney to Loughborough to the Grammar School.

Michael was different: he was a happy-go-lucky child, worked hard at the things he liked, but had the knack of avoiding the jobs he disliked. Now he wishes he had worked harder at those things. He tells his own son where he went wrong and tries to persuade him to learn from his father's mistakes. But this boy, Brian, is a chip off the old block and goes his own sweet way. Still I feel quite sure he will find his feet somewhere successfully.

While the war lasted, children had little more toys and entertainment than in my generation. They, too, had to make their own pleasures. Sidney and David found an old pram, they took off the body, and with four perfectly good wheels, they made a trolley. They had a good run for this game, as our stack yard and driveway went down quite a steep hill all the way from the fields, but it was rough going. When the weather was fine and the ground was dry, it was quite good, but there was no tarmac on this ground and in bad weather it was quite often a quagmire. After a time, the boys thought they might try the trolley on Wysall Lane which was twice as long and offered a much smoother ride, but at the bottom it entered the main road and traffic was a problem.

One day Sidney and David were on the trolley, with Sidney driving and David sitting at the back. They were halfway down the hill, going at a terrific speed, when they heard a motor car coming down the lane behind them. Sidney lost control of the trolley which went into speed wobbles and finally ran into a bank at the side of the road. It turned upside down with the wheels spinning furiously, one of which cut into the fleshy part of David's calf, making a nasty deep cut which required seven stitches. When Sidney looked at this huge gaping wound, he thought part of the flesh was missing and surreptitiously went back to the scene of the accident to find the missing piece. He was quite upset when he could not find it and much relieved when told there was no flesh missing and that the wound would be quite alright when the doctor had stitched it up. I sat in horrified silence as the doctor stitched this gaping wound without any anaesthetic.

Young Michael, at the age of three, went with his father to mend a fence. Mischievously he picked up a very sharp saw to play with, finishing up by falling on it and cutting a huge gash across the palm of his hand. I picked him up and rushed him to the doctor, who said that Michael did not need a stitch, as binding the hand into a clenched fist would heal it nicely. I was pleased about this, but Michael was much perturbed because he was unable to suck his thumb, a thing he did even in the daytime. At night he could not sleep without his thumb and kept crying: "I can't suck my fum, Mummy." I said: "Suck your other thumb, then." "No, no," he cried, "it doesn't taste the same."

One summer's evening, when Michael was around eleven years old, he disappeared. I was deeply worried, becoming even more so as the dark hour approached. After frantic, fruitless searching, I began to think of obtaining police help, when just before eleven o'clock he sauntered into the yard with a teenage boy who worked on our farm. My anger at his answer to my agitated question as to where he had been knew no bounds. I berated Michael and punished him harder than I should have, being very sorry afterwards. They had been fishing.

When Sydney and David were in their teenage years, Sid and I noticed an advert in a Nottingham paper offering a half-sized billiard table for sale. Sid was a good billiard player and he thought how nice it would be for the boys and their friends to be able to learn to play this game in our own home. We set forth to Nottingham, fixing the trailer to our car in case we bought the table. We found it in new condition. Sid did not hesitate in clinching the deal, and that night the table was fixed and both Sid and the boys, along with many of their friends, were playing at every available opportunity. I found great pleasure in watching them play, but never mind how I tried, I was no good at all at the game. I used to practice on my own but I never got any better. Sid said I was hopeless, and after a while I gave up, realizing I had no aptitude for the game.

At all our parties the sexes became divided, the ladies gossiping in the sitting room and the men playing or watching the billiards.

I consider my children were lucky to grow up on a farm. Right from my childhood days, I have felt sorry for town children, many of whom never see an animal apart from cats and dogs. We had some neighbours whose town relatives visited them from time to time. Once one of the children came to our farm when it was milking time. He stood in the doorway transfixed. "Ooer," he cried, "we don't get our milk from a dirty old cow, we buy ours in a bottle!" One can imagine my children's disdainful look at this child who did not even know that his milk came from a cow. I remember with great amusement Sid telling me a story about this same boy when he stood about three yards away, watching a cow being milked by hand. Sid said to the boy: "Close your eyes and open your mouth wide", then he accurately squirted a stream of milk straight into the boy's mouth. He spat and spluttered the milk out of his mouth shouting: "I don't want milk from a dirty old cow, it's awful."

When I was a child, village children rarely visited a town and town children visited the country only when they had relatives living there.

12 MY BROTHERS AND
   SID'S SISTER

During the war all my brothers were in the building trade, which was a reserved occupation. Nearly all private building was discontinued, and only necessary repair work was allowed. My eldest brother, Warner, worked on the new aerodrome at Wymeswold in a building capacity.

The middle brother, John, was eager to join one of the forces, so he left the building trade and took a job as a taxi driver. While John was doing this work, he met and fell in love with an Irish girl named Sally Quinn who worked in Loughborough as a dentist's receptionist. This wartime friendship developed quickly and they were married, finding rooms in Loughborough. Accommodation was hard to obtain during the war. John was eventually called up and was sent with the Navy to India. Sally kept on her receptionist's job. At one time she lived with a lady hairdresser, whom she occasionally helped out at busy times. Sally developed an interest in hairdressing, becoming most proficient at this work.

After the war, in his spare time, John built a bungalow on London Lane in Wymeswold and Sally built up a hairdressing business. She permed and looked after nearly all her friends' and relations' hair, doing a marvellous job.

Sadly, this happy life was not to continue, for after a very happy marriage Sally became seriously ill with cancer. She had an operation which was thought to have been successful in clearing this dreadful disease, but after a while its signs began to show again. After all known treatment had been given, it became clear to those who loved her that she would not recover. Her fortitude and faith that she would eventually get better were a wonder and a lesson to those who nursed her. Sally had many friends, especially one who travelled ten miles two or three days each week to help nurse her. The Wootton family formed a rota, so that Sally was never left alone until John came home from work, then he took over the night duty.

Our sister Edna came to visit us from London. When she went to see Sally, Sally asked her if she would like her to do her hair. "Go and wash it and I will set it for you," said Sally, and this she did with Edna sitting on the floor before her. This was the last time Sally did anyone's hair, and a few weeks later her indomitable spirit was stilled and she died.

John and Sally never had any children and John never re-married. After Sally died, I always thought that John helped himself through his grief by helping other people. He spent as much time as he could helping others and doing little kind acts. He was always there to take anyone into hospital, fetch them out, or convey visitors in his car to see patients.

He had a course of cookery lessons and managed extremely well with the help of our sister Lottie. For a number of years he made several pork pies each week, delivering two to old age pensioners in the village, a whole pie for a married couple and a half for a single person. This kindly deed was much appreciated by the old folk and John enjoyed visiting and talking to them. It was after dark hour one night, when he knocked at an old lady's door and she shouted: "Go away, I'm not opening that door to anyone after it's dark." "All right," John shouted back, "I shall have to give someone else your half of a pork pie." John always smiled when he told anyone this story. He said he had never seen a door open so quickly, and the old lady literally pulled him inside.

My youngest brother, William, who was the joiner in the family building firm, was also in a reserved occupation. When the war broke out, he wanted to join the air force. He went for his medical but, much to his surprise and chagrin, did not pass A1, as there was a certain weakness left from when he had scarlet fever. He was told this would not affect him while living a normal life, but he could not stand up to the rigours of war. Bill suggested to the examiners that a recent bout of flu might explain the disorder, so was told to try again after three months, but the second verdict was the same. Being in the reserved occupation of building and not gaining the required A1 pass, Bill was refused admission into the forces, so he also took a job helping to build the airmen's living quarters on the aerodrome.

While he was thus occupied, he met and fell in love with a pretty teenage farmer's daughter named Phillis Copley who lived in Nottinghamshire but worked in a Loughborough shop. By the time they were twenty-one, they were married and went to live with our parents in Wymeswold. Phyllis continued her work in Loughborough until their baby girl Margaret was born. After a few weeks they came to live with Sid and myself at our farm. Bill cut a doorway between the sitting-room and our bottom cellar. The cellar floor was built up to a suitable level and a kitchenette was made. This allowed the young couple a complete little home of their own: they used the front door and staircase and we used the back door and back staircase.

My youngest son Michael and baby Margaret grew up to be almost inseparable, getting into all kinds of scrapes together. Once my father, who was then around seventy years old, had spent all of one day making a long concrete path across our front garden. He was very tired when the job was finished, so he came into the house for a tot of whisky. The children were playing outside, when Dad suddenly said: "You don't think, Nell, that those kids'll walk on my wet concrete?" I answered: "I don't think they would, Dad, but I'll nip out and have a look." Oh, my goodness, the two of them had chased up and down, up and down that wet concrete path. At one end where out soot heap had been piled under a lilac tree, the had run through the soot each time. What a mess! The children were filthy, but one can imagine the state of Dad's smooth concrete path, blackened and churned by sooty footprints. When Dad came out after drinking his whisky, he exclaimed: "The naughty little buggers!" But he cheerfully got down on his knees, scraped off the

soot, wet the concrete and smoothed it off again. In spite of the children's pranks, we spent four happy years together, helping each other. We would baby sit one for the other when we had a little outing. Towards the end of their stay with us, Bill and Phyll had another little girl who was named Judith.

Living so happily together, we enjoyed many amusing incidents, like one morning when Bill came into our part of the house saying: "Nell, there is a mouse in our bedroom." I said: "Such rubbish, Bill. We've never had a mouse in our farmhouse." "Well," says Bill, "we have now, I can hear noises behind our wardrobe." Now Sid, who loved a joke, thought about a very realistic toy mouse that had been given to Michael. That evening he surreptitiously crept into Bill and Phyll's bedroom, made a dent in Bill's pillow, and placed into it the toy mouse. Bill was extremely conscious of the intruding mouse in their bedroom and was on the lookout for it. Consequently, when he saw the furry mouse sitting snugly on his pillow, he made a great dive for it. There was great fun, but one can imagine the language when he found out he had been tricked and the mouse was not real.

When Bill told us we had a mouse upstairs, I immediately thought of a half- hundredweight bag of best white flour which I kept in the lumber room. Not much had been used, as we only used white flour for the pork pies and special occasions. We knew this would be the last white flour we would be able to buy until after the war was over. Meantime we could get only a coarse brown flour. I raced to the lumber room where, to my dismay, this very precious bag of flour was full of mice and their droppings and the whole room stank of mice. I could have cried to think of this ruined flour so carefully rationed. Those beastly mice had crept up the outside wall and burrowed their way through a weak joint, then through the inside wall plaster. I could not help wondering how the mice knew there was this flour upstairs, as we had never had a mouse in the house before. Also, how on earth did they find the nearest way to obtain an entrance to the upstairs room through a double brick wall? They made only one small hole and I often tried to imagine that army of mice creeping one by one in the dead of night, up the wall, through that tiny hole and plop, into my special bag of white flour. How I hated giving it to our pigs but my, didn't they enjoy it mixed into their poor ration! Ah well, it's an ill wind that blows nobody good!

A matter of days before the war ended, we received the dreadful news that Sid's sister Kathleen's husband, Johnno, had been killed in Holland. He was in a jeep with one of his superior officers, driving along a main road, when a lorry came straight out of a side road, hitting the jeep broadside. Johnno was thrown out and killed instantly. The news came just after Kathleen had left for her teaching job in Loughborough. Her father came to the farm to tell us the awful news, which struck us all numb with shock. Father said he could not possibly tell Kath, and asked Sid and me tell her. We agreed, although it was the hardest thing we ever had to do. We quietly prepared ourselves, leaving the children with their grandfather. Our journey to Loughborough was taken in almost complete silence. We arrived at the Grammar School where Kath was a teacher and asked to see the headmaster. He was very upset, as Johnno had been a master at the school for a number of years. Much to our relief, he broke the sad news to Kathleen, who could not believe it, for she had received several letters from Johnno that morning. We took Kathleen home, but after a short time the headmaster persuaded her to return to work. Kathleen said she would never forget the kindness he and his wife showed her during that sad time.

13 TIMES CHANGE

The war against Germany ended in May, and against Japan in August 1945. The Peace Rejoicings took place in our village, with the band playing, followed by a huge procession, with everyone in fancy dress. A tea was given, everyone being welcomed. Like everywhere else in the country, there was a great sadness mixed with the relief and happiness that at long last the war was over. It was many years before life became normal once again.

Ration books remained with us for a long time, but foods like bananas gradually started coming into our country once again. Some children had never seen a banana. I well remember the first bunch I bought. I was giving my children one each, the older ones peeling their own. The two youngest, I thought, would not be able to manage, so I told my three-year old niece to hold hers while I peeled young Michael's. When I turned to help her, the banana had disappeared. I said: "Barbara, where have you put your banana?" She answered: "I have eaten it, Auntie." "But where have you put the skin, dear?" I asked. "One has to be careful not to leave banana skins where people will slip on them." "Oh, Auntie, I have eaten that as well. I thought you ate it all!" she replied.

After the war there were many more cars on the roads, whereas, during our early years, there had been only three cars in our village. They were owned by Dr Tawse, an ear, nose and throat specialist who lived at Wymeswold Hall and travelled to Nottingham each day, Mr John Burrows, who owned a large farm, and Mr John James, a farmer butcher. The rest of us used a horse and float or bicycles for getting around.

One remembers the journeys we used to make and the fun we used to have on our bicycles, taking risks which we would be horrified to

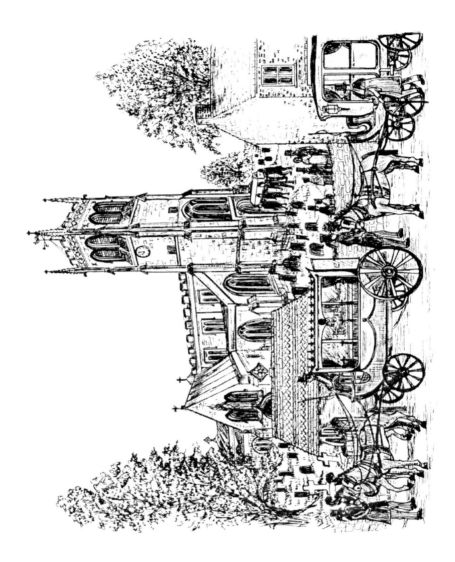

think our grandchildren might take. Bicycles helped in cases of illness, too. One old lady in the village became ill and needed to be hospitalized for the rest of her life. She had no relatives to help, so when the ambulance came, I was asked to help carry her downstairs and to travel with her to the hospital, which was around six or seven miles the other side of Loughborough. Because of petrol rationing, the ambulance would not be allowed to bring me home, so we decided to take my bicycle with us in the ambulance and I would cycle home. I had not cycled for many months because of pregnancy and the birth of my child whom I was still breastfeeding. After we had left the old lady, I managed the first half a dozen miles home without feeling any effect. Then the muscles of my legs and thighs began to ache. A few more miles and they absolutely seized up, and I was forced to rest for a consider-able time. I began to worry, as it was several hours past my baby's feed time. Sid's mother was looking after the baby and I knew she would be worrying too. I finished that journey walking like an old woman of ninety. I was just as ravenously hungry as my baby, so I just rinsed my hands and face, sat down in a comfortable chair, and fed my baby while eating my dinner which Grandma Smith handed me.

Bicycles were quite often used in emergencies and nearly everyone cycled to work. When I was a child, one of my greatest delights was to meet my father coming home on his bicycle: he would sit me on his handlebars and ride me the rest of the way home.

Cricket, bowls and tennis teams used bicycles as well as horses and floats to convey them to play other village teams. It was a common Saturday afternoon sight to see the young ones riding four abreast, holding their tennis racquets in one hand and steering their bicycles with the other.

Sometimes at our sports affairs they had a slow bicycle race. It needed quite a lot of practice to keep one's seat without falling off, but several of the village boys were marvellous and entertained us all with their prowess.

At the age of seventy-odd years, my grandfather bought a great tricycle. We kids watched him mount, then start to pedal, and we howled with laughter as he lost control of the steering, climbed a bank, then fell backwards. Grandfather allowed us kids to try to ride this tricycle, but each one of us finished up in the hedge. We had tremendous fun, but none realized how difficult it was to ride a trike.

When I was a child, the thing that saddened us most was a death in the village. Everyone knew everyone else so, when a death occurred, many people attended the funeral in sympathy for the relatives and respect for the one who had passed away. The schoolmaster used to take out into the playground the forms we sat on in school, allowing us children to stand on them to see over the school wall and pay our respects, as the cortege entered the churchyard opposite. We always had strict instructions to behave in a manner suitable for such a sad occasion. I do not think that warning was necessary, as the sight of the coffin in the hearse, drawn by two magnificent black horses, followed by several cabs, also drawn by black horses, was a magnificent but awesome sight. Most of the children cried. I know I did. What's more, I always looked up into the sky to see if I could see the dead person's spirit ascending into heaven, as we were taught in our scripture lessons to believe that this was what happened when we died. I was always so disappointed not to see this sight, although I had no idea what a spirit should look like.

During the first few years of my life, several old people were buried in either the churchyard or the Baptist Chapel cemetery, but eventually these places became full and then all the burials took place at the cemetery situated on the Rempstone Lane. A small chapel had been built in the middle of the cemetery, but this building was seldom used, and as the years rolled on, it gradually deteriorated. Vandals broke the windows and the rain caused more damage. At last the building was demolished, leaving a desolate-looking empty space. Some of the Wymeswold residents regretted the demolition of this ancient building, but damp and vandals made its pulling down necessary.

We had in the village a structure that few other villages had. It was a circular wall of red bricks around six feet high with a strong wooden gate and it was called a compound. Its original purpose was to shut up stray animals, but it was never used as far as I knew, because the gate was always locked and only a few people knew where the key was kept.

This enclosure stood at the bottom of Stalkard Lane, which was a deeply-rutted road leading to a lonely farmhouse. These ruts became so deep that people used to take their old tins and rubbish to help fill them in. A deep dyke on one side of the lane was also used for this purpose. If all that was dug up now, one would expect to find a treasure trove of antiquities thrown away all those years ago.

It was not only in machinery, electricity and water, that farming advanced. We were quite amazed when artificial insemination gradually took over the natural way of extending our herds. At first Sid would not make use of this artificial method and still had our cows served with either our own bull or our neighbour's bull. The neighbour's bull was a huge Hereford, which begat very large calves. Then the farmers realized that getting these huge calves was not all to the good. Our cows, like those of other farmers, began having difficulty in delivering their calves. I remember two cases of our own, when the calf was much too big to be born and we had to fetch the vet. In both cases the vet had to cut them away from the mother bit by bit. I watched him perform this awful operation on one of our young heifers. He used a wire for cutting, not a knife. After these two hard calvings, Sid relented and always used the artificial insemination method thereafter. Nowadays, it is the general practice.

Milking has also become very specialized. Instead of every farmer having a small herd and pushing the milk into the cheese factory in a churn fixed to wheels, a huge tanker lorry now calls at a few specialized farms, where everything is absolutely up to the standards set by the Milk Marketing Board. As these standards were extremely high, the small farmers were unable to afford the terrific costs of modernizing their premises, and during the course of a few years, they were forced out of milking.

Many farmers, including my two farmer sons, ploughed up all their land and converted their cowsheds into piggeries. These small farmers did quite well with pigs for a few years but soon over-production caused severe financial losses. Many farmers who stuck with pigs, hoping for better times which did not come, went bankrupt. One farmer told me he was losing between five and six pounds on each pig he fattened. A farmer could not possibly stand this type of loss for very long. Neither of my sons keep pigs any more.

A pleasant country sight, that one rarely sees nowadays, is the herd of milking cows coming down the lane to the farm to be milked. Some people regret this, but others, especially car- and lorry-drivers welcome the change, as a herd of cows can cause terrific traffic jams. Drovers that used to muster all the farmer's cattle together to walk them to market either retired or became cattle-truck drivers and cattle trucks became a common sight on our roads.

In those days we had a great deal of fun with our horses, daring each other in various ways. Many people, who have little or no experience with horses, think some of the exploits we indulged in were cruel to the horses but, believe me, most of the horses I knew just loved the games we played. One horse we had, named Bob, knew and loved the game of musical chairs. We used to practice this game in the home field with some of us singing. This horse knew that as soon as the music stopped, he had to turn and race towards the nearest box.

When one is young, a gallop on a horse without a saddle and with a halter in place of a bridle, with only one's knees to guide it, is the most gloriously exhilarating feeling one could ever wish to experience. I myself enjoyed doing this, even when I was too small to mount without help, but where there is a will, there is always a way.

I used to draw the horse alongside a gate, climb the gate, and jump on to the horse's back and away I would go. The horse knew this manoeuvre as well as I did and would almost place himself, waiting patiently while I climbed the gate.

One particular feat that Sid's brother Bob learned to do while in his teens involved the two heavy horses. Having them in readiness for a day's ploughing, he would stand behind them with the reins round his arms, then make a gigantic spring, with a hand on each horse's flank, and land with a foot on each one's back. He would then proceed at a gentle trot up the lane, looking exactly like a circus rider. Sid was quite envious of young Bob's prowess and he became quite determined to do the same. In spite of being eight years older and of a much thicker build, he at last managed to emulate his kid brother. He said to me one morning: "Nell, watch me out of the yard and you will see I can do the circus act just as well as our young Bob." Much to my surprise he did, but never quite so elegantly as Bob.

Horses love hunting. My brother Warner rode a mare to hounds once or twice, after which, if the mare was in a field and the hunt was anywhere near, she would jump the hedge and follow the meet without a rider. Whenever we knew the huntsmen were around, we had to shut her up in the stable, but she still got terribly excited when she heard them. Even in these modern times of television, one can see how the horses love jumping by just looking at their pricked ears and eager demeanour.

I look back on those happy days with horses and regret their passing, but one has to live with the times, and I am the first to admit that, at the age of seventy-six, I am extremely happy to be still driving a car. From my window I watch my grandchild, Julia, putting her horse through its paces in the home field, and I thank God for times past and for my ever-growing family of grand-children.